First published in 2005 by MBI, an imprint of MBI Publishing Company, Galtier Plaza, Suite 200, 380 Jackson Street, St. Paul, MN 55101-3885 USA

MBI titles are also available at discounts in bulk quantity for industrial or sales-promotional use. For details write to Special Sales Manager at MBI Publishing Company, Galtier Plaza, Suite 200, 380 Jackson Street, St. Paul, MN 55101-3885 USA.

ISBN 0-7603-1794-1

Editor: Amy Glaser
Designer: Suzi Hutsell

Printed in China

Frontispiece: Bowling magazines, which were usually written by men, advised women on slim and sexy styles that brought out curvaceous lines thanks to short skirts and tight blouses. Fiddlesticks! Women wore outrageous outfits thanks to this newfound freedom given to them by bowling. If men could have glitzy bowling shirts, why couldn't women?

Title page: Sid Southard shows how to roll a perfect game by looking down the alley. *Shellum Bowling Hall of Fame*

Back cover (left): This AMF promo photo showed how the most modern alleys offered nurseries to look after Junior while Mama bowls. Beware of any daycare that offers heavy wooden pins to toddlers as a toy!

Back cover (right): Dropping down in the pit to steady the pins, these adolescent pinboys pose for a photo in 1909 at the Arcade Bowling Alley in Trenton, New Jersey. Notice the duck pins in lanes 5 and 6.

contents

The eternal struggle between pinboy and bowler satisfies two innate human needs: to create and destroy. Just as Hannibal helped erect Carthage, the Romans knocked it down only to rebuild it again. Achilles leveled Troy with his clever horse and went home with a medal: Helen, his trophy wife. What goes up, must come down. The phoenix burns in flames of glory, only to rise again from the ashes.

Bowlers take this human condition into their hands when they step on the approach with their Brunswick ball in their hands. Dry that hand of any sweat and insert three fingers in the holes. One, two, three, four steps; the shoe slides; the wrist is tight; and the ball is let go toward its crashing destiny. The bowler is like Atlas, dropping his world to test his fate at rolling a perfect game. And so the earth-shaped sphere plummets down the maple alley with deafening speed, avoiding the abyss on either side of the lane.

When a split seems imminent—behold!—a last-minute hook sends this black ball into the pocket between the 1 and 3 pins. The white-and-red woodpile scatters in every direction. Kismet! The sweet pleasure of sweeping the pins from their feet with a single ball inspires a victory dance, just as rolling a gutterball may enrage an otherwise placid bowler to stoop to new levels of blasphemy. Triumph is nothing without having once been in the dregs, throwing sour apples. At some point all of us are in the gutter, but some are looking at the stars. Rolling a cherry and splitting the pins is a half-won battle. Only a rematch will lead to victory—if that damn ball return will just hurry up.

Just as Sisyphus rolled his rock up the hill for the rest of eternity, pinboys were condemned to set up the lumber and roll back the ball for more punishment. As though relieved of their toil by a benevolent god, pinboys were put out of a job by AMF and Brunswick's automatic pinsetters. Much as John Henry fought the steam drill, modern bowlers continue this perpetual cycle of splashing the pins only to see them set up by a machine. With 95 million bowlers worldwide, this battle to topple pins continues every minute of every day. Right now, somewhere, someone is bowling.

So, the clash continues "in this mortal coil." This fight between being and nothingness, between clearing the pins and seeing them set up perfectly again. The battle between rolling 300 and splitting the pins.

Any guerrilla warfare is kosher in bowling, from locked-elbow shuffling to humble granny-style rolling. As the pins are shattered, no one may laugh. Bowlers of any size may play—from a skin-and-bones waif to a bowling-ball-shaped Sumo wrestler. Any race may roll—from Anglo-Saxon aristocrats to world-record-setting Filipinos. Any class may bowl—from rabble-rousing proletariat to flush fat cats. This is bowling. The great equalizer that knocks down barriers with each strike rolled. The great gatherer that brings together more people than any other game. The great sport and humble hobby that conquered the world. *Now, let's roll...*

GIVES YOU POSITIVE ACTION WITH EACH BALL YOU ROLL!

Chapter One

BOWLING THROUGHOUT TIME

Creative bowling historians have traced the origin of bowling to the world's greatest civilizations. Polynesians bowled with rounded stones and rock pins in a game named Ula Maika. Although the length of the lane measured 60 feet—nearly identical to the 62 feet of modern alleys—Ula Maika can't be directly traced to Western ten-pin bowling.

British explorer and anthropologist Sir Flinders Petrie traveled to Egypt in the 1930s in hopes of seizing a pharaoh's fortune. Thanks to hired hands, Sir Petrie began digging through an ancient burial site dating from between 3200 to 5200 B.C. Rather than unearthing Tutankhamen's tomb or other booty to be brought to the British Museum, he discovered a child's bowling game.

Another expedition in 2002 by archaeologists from the University of Pisa to Medinet Madi in Al Fayum, Egypt, revealed a similar find. An early mix of bowling and croquet, the uncovered child's game involved setting up nine marble obelisks. Then a teenaged Egyptian rolled a rounded stone down a groove under a wicket to topple the pins. The Italian scientists concurred with Sir Petrie that bowling could stand next to the Sphinx and the Great Pyramid of Giza as another great Egyptian contribution to humanity.

Perhaps questioning that Mark Anthony and Cleopatra spent their free time rolling a line, the scholar Wolfgang Decker doubts the theory that bowling spread from Egypt to Greece in 2000 B.C. (and therefore the earliest Olympic Games), on to Rome, and eventually to America. In his erudite *Sports and Games of Ancient Egypt*, Decker explained after years of research, "The adventuresome thesis that all modern ball games derive

NEW AMSTERDAM Painter Mort Luby portrays the bowling green on the southern tip of Manhattan. Most likely these Dutch bowlers played nine-pin skittles with a taller kingpin in the middle. Today the windmill is gone, but the park remains as a memorial to the first bowling pitch in the country. *Mort Luby*

from the games once played in the Nile Valley in the days of the pharaohs...has been shown to be erroneous."

Not to be foiled by naysayers, bowling historians regrouped and Carol Schunk proposed a new hypothesis in her book, *Bowling*: "The Romans did much of their fighting in hilly areas, so one of their tactical maneuvers was to roll rocks down a pass to attract or bowl over their oncoming enemy. The soldiers practiced to develop skill in this tactic and before long began to 'play' this game for fun." According to Schunk's theory, Roman centurions throughout the Pax Romana spread this warlike game during the time of Christ.

An expert in social aspects of Roman life who holds a Ph.D. in classical studies from the University of Minnesota, Dr. Mark Vesley rebuts, "The story about bowling coming from Romans dropping rocks on Christians for sport is an antique urban legend. Sure, they'd roll or drop boulders on enemies during wartime...but similarity doesn't prove derivation. The ball games played in Rome usually used a sort of medicine ball, often an inflatable goat's bladder, thrown back and forth. Rather than bowling in the Coliseum to kill Christians, they used more conventional means, like lions or having them hack each other apart."

Unable to definitely trace their sport to empires of old, the International Bowling Hall of Fame and Museum in St. Louis, Missouri, chalks up the origin of bowling to an innate human trait. The first exhibit of the museum features a caveman mannequin grasping a stone and the text, "The beginning of bowling. Is this how bowling began with a stone-age hunter tossing a rock at a formation of bones? No one is sure. What we do know is that bowling is one of the oldest types of games still being played."

THE PHARAOH'S GAME Hieroglyphics dating from 1490 to 1436 B.C. reveal the (unlikely) possibility that Tuthmosis III bowled at the Temple of Hatshepsut in Egypt.

For skeptics of this evolution, Joe Falcaro wrote his Creationist theory in *Bowling for All*: "[S]ome historians even ponder on the possibility that the boys in the Garden of Eden used to throw giant pebbles at a lineup of pointed stones." Bowling was a God-given pleasure.

Striking Down the Devil

While scholars may have debunked theories such as that advocated in *The Woman's Bowling Guide* ("Northern Italy saw bowling in the time of the Caesars"), Italian lawn bowling, or *bocce*, dates back at least to the Middle Ages. As the perfect outdoor sport to play while building an appetite for lunch, bocce reached throughout the Riviera and became known as *petanque* in France. With the popularity of this pastime, rumors spread that a stash of golden bocce balls was being hoarded and guarded by demons in a castle tower somewhere in the boot of Italy.

Tracing bowling to bocce is dubious, however, because Italian lawn bowling has no pins. Curiously, Italians mixed their lawn bowling with billiards. *Boccette* (little bocce) is played on a pocketless pool table and the ball is rolled by hand. Another derivation is played with miniature pins called *birilli* that are about 1 inch in height and are placed in a diamond pattern in the

NOBLE LAWN BOWLING The idle rich take time out from the pub to bowl on the green in Elizabethan England. The postmark on this card is from Kansas and dates back to 1913.

454. Bowling.

center of the table. A pool cue banks the ball to tumble as many pins as possible in this game called Goriziana, after Gorizia, the northeast region of Italy.

Not content with Italy receiving all the credit for bowling, the Grimm Brothers sought to trace the history of the game to their native Germany. After penning their frightening fairy tales, the Grimms employed their fantasy to assert that early Teutonic tribes made an offering to the king of the gods, Wodan, by bowling down pins before hunting for meat.

Historian and fellow German, William Pehle, took up the Grimms' cause and claimed that German bowling dates back to A.D. 300 during the waning years of the Caesars. Visigoths and Ostrogoths favored the bowling ball for battle—an argument already made for the Romans—and possibly rolled them during the sacking of Rome.

British scholars trace German bowling back to one of their own countrymen named Winfrid who exported the game when he converted the Saxon tribes to Christianity around A.D. 700. Winfrid sanctified bowling by proclaiming that the "kegel," or pin, was actually the "heide," or devil. With each pin knocked over, another demon was killed and another victory could be chalked up for Christ. The pagans struck back, however, by bludgeoning the poor priest while he confirmed a new batch of converts. After his death in 754, Winfrid was canonized as St. Boniface and became the de facto Patron Saint of Bowling.

St. Boniface was martyred, but his bowling legacy lived on in Germany. Well into the thirteenth century, monks and priests from Haberstadt to Magdeburg bowled over the devil to pay homage to Boniface and "celebrate the victory of Christianity over paganism," according to the International Bowling Hall of Fame and Museum.

The obsession with bowling soon gave this sacred sport a bad reputation. Austrian fables reasoned that noise from the hills must be pesky dwarves bowling in caves with silver and gold balls. Soon even Satan himself was seen bowling. While Christians knocked over the devil with each roll, Lucifer struck back by bowling a human skull to shatter Christ's cross. The eye sockets and single nose hole provided a nice three-holed ball similar to modern designs.

Bowling received another negative blow and became a curse to high-minded puritans. When 1,400 miners drowned in a flooded mine shaft in Austria in 1360, the priests reasoned that God was punishing the workers for wasting time bowling. To keep medieval judges in line, a myth was circulated that if an innocent man was condemned to death, the judge had to spend his afterlife bowling with the victims' severed heads. A man of the cloth who didn't follow Christ's example must spend eternity bowling. A curse to some, but a wish come true for others.

Bowling was so popular in Germany that keglers (bowlers) staked their livestock—from horses to oxen—on the outcome of a single game. In an attempt to eradicate gambling, the government in Frankfurt banned bowling in 1443 and 1447. After angry keglers took to the streets in protest in 1468, bowling was back, but only small wagers were allowed.

Just as Martin Luther cleaned up the Christian church by nailing his 95 Theses on the door of the Wittenberg Castle Church, he also cleaned up the game of bowling. During bowling's reformation in the 1500s, Luther set the rules for the sport and declared that exactly nine pins should be used in a proper game. Luther succumbed to the temptation of bowling and liked it so much he indulged his family with a private alley.

The Game of Kings

Apart from St. Boniface, British bowling extends back at least until 1100 when Parliament passed a law banning the game because it was becoming more popular than the national sport of archery. In 1366, King Edward III is said to have outlawed bowling in his army because his archers would rather roll than shoot arrows, thus putting the nation in peril. Edward's archers likely bowled on the

SATAN'S SKULLDUGGERY
Toppling pins was the same as knocking down the Devil, according to Saint Boniface. Soon, bowling cast a spell on weak-minded bowlers who couldn't resist leaving work to roll a line and gamble a bit. Bans on bowling called it an infernal game and the word was Satan himself flattened crosses with his bowling ball, which had three holes: two eye sockets and a nose hole.

"A POODLE." Copyright, 1905, by U. Co., N. Y.

Copyright, 1907, by U. Co., N. Y. "A STRIKE."

CORPULENT KEGLERS Early humorous postcards from 1907 depicted hefty robber barons taking off their greatcoats and rolling balls between a puff of a cigar and swig of cognac. *Shellum Bowling Hall of Fame collection*

lawn at Crown Greene in Southampton, England, which is a bowling green still in use today. Another ancient alley—perhaps the world's oldest "skittle" lane, The Sheep Head Inn, in Edinburgh, Scotland—was frequented by James the Sixth and Mary Queen of Scots as early as 1360. A "skittle" is another name for a slender pin, and the game of skittles is usually a nine-pin game with the pins set up in a diamond pattern.

Bowling's biggest advocate in Britain was Henry VIII. In between marrying and sometimes beheading his six wives, Henry had an indoor nine-pin alley built at his Whitehall Palace in 1532. Henry disapproved of bowling for the masses and declared that a minimum annual income of £1,000 was required to roll. Bowling became an elite endeavor and only royalty or the wealthy could play. Henry gambled and lost vast amounts of royal treasure, particularly to the Duke of Norfolk, on bowling.

In the summer of 1588, after sailing around the world, Sir Francis Drake returned to Great Britain and was bowling on the green when a frantic messenger rode up and announced the impending arrival of Spain's "Invincible Armada" to avenge Drake's plundering of Spanish settlements in the New World. As the story

SCORECARD POSTCARD Rather than relying on dusty chalkboards to mark strikes and spares, this handy postcard of bowlers with oversized heads offered a scorecard for a team of five. *Shellum Bowling Hall of Fame collection*

THE WORLD'S OLDEST ALLEY?

"You bob the ball between your legs then take a great big Superman dive to get closer to the pins," the barkeep of the Sheep Head Inn in Edinburgh tells me when describing how to play ten-pin skittles Scottish style. The ball is approximately the same size as an average ten-pin ball but has no holes, ergo the granny-style roll spiced with strapping Caledonian brawn.

"The game is similar to rugby in that you launch yourself forward to throw the ball and land on your belly. It's a bit taxing," Scotsman Euan Kerr recalls of his skittle bowling days. "Then some poor soul at the end of the alley has to keep setting up the pins!"

The medieval Sheep Head Inn has few updates, but does boast a relatively modern ball return dating back to the 1880s when the "Trotters Club" would meet. This social gathering of lawyers, artists, and poets, congregated to bowl, discuss Diderot, drink a pint, and sing songs about skittles.

The Sheep Head Inn (pronounced and sometimes spelled "Sheep Heid Inn") is the oldest pub in Scotland, dating back to 1360. "Mary Queen of Scots visited, as did Richard Nixon," the barkeep continues. "I'm not sure if ol' Dick bowled though. Perhaps he was afraid of lunging on to the floor for a better score."

Mary Queen of Scots' son, James VI, used to pop by the pub when passing from one Edinburgh palace to the next. When not writing on witchcraft or expounding on the divine right of kings, James bowled skittles in the yard around 1575 to 1580. He was so pleased with the pub that he bestowed upon it a severed ram's head embossed with gold and silver and filled with ground tobacco. "It's called a 'snuff mull,'" says owner D. J. Johnston-Smith. "We have an imitation now, and the original sheep's head is probably sitting in some country estate somewhere and they don't know what they have." The inn named for this gruesome gift can now boast being the oldest skittle alley in the world.

HEAVIEST BOWLING TEAM IN AMERICA.

HEAVIEST BOWLING TEAM IN AMERICA Showing off their matching bowling uniforms and bulbous bellies, this hefty team with bowling ball–shaped bodies hailed from downtown Saint Paul, Minnesota. *Minnesota Historical Society*

STRAPPING SPORTSMEN Don't forget your top hat and overcoat before witnessing the latest stalwart bowler dressed in early boxing garb. Notice the poor pinboy above the pit. *Shellum Bowling Hall of Fame collection*

goes, Drake calmed the panicky messenger with classic British *sang-froid* and continued playing—and winning—his game before defeating the conquistadors at the Battle of Gravelines.

For a while in the sixteenth century, bowling was viewed as a moral and upright sport. Nobleman Francis Bacon extolled the virtues of the sport in his collection *Essays or Counsels: Civil and Moral* from 1597 by advising his readers, "Bowling is good for the stone and reins [kidneys]."

Once again, bowling's reputation was sullied by extravagant gambling. The devout King James decreed that after Sunday mass, good Christians should not be "disturbed, letted, or discouraged" by bowling of "the meaner sort of people." In response to the bans on this once-divine pastime, inventive British peasants devised a game sarcastically dubbed "The Bubble of Justice" with nine little holes where the pins once stood. It wasn't until 1845 that the British royalty declared commoners could once again indulge in bowling.

In the 1300s, France banned bowling "because of gambling rowdiness...men's delinquency from jobs, families, and military training." Nevertheless, French farmers anted up with one chicken before a game of *quilles de neuf* (nine pins), *carreau*, or *quatre coins* (four corners), in which they traded off rolling the *fromage*, so named because the ball looked like a cheese wheel. The winner took all the chickens home—at least until the next village tournament.

Neither Gallic priests nor nobles needed to worry about a *gendarme* breaking down their door for illicit bowling. While Cardinal Richelieu was busy consolidating power in the 1600s, Louis XIII and other royalty dressed in their velvet robes, frilly lace, and powdered periwigs to bowl on the lawn of the Fontainebleau chateau. The wily Richelieu knew that absolute power corrupts absolutely but

also that bowling distracts an absolute ruler. Richelieu could enact his silent coup d'état while Louis XIII tried to pick up a split. Once again the proverb was proved: "A king would rather bowl than rule."

New World of Bowling

While the English and French royalty were busy bowling on their manors, the Dutch colonized New Netherland with their nine-pin skittles. In 1626, a Dutch governor named Peter Minuit famously bought a lush island at the

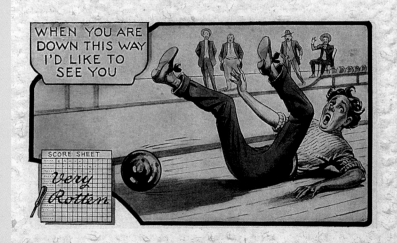

BOWLING POSTCARDS Many early bowling postcards had printed black-and-white photos of famous bowlers, such as Hank Marino and Andy Varipapa. Corny wordplay, bad puns, and slightly naughty joke cards were passed around on league night or sent across country. Christmas and Valentine's Day bowling cards came next and were followed by free glossy advertising postcards for bowling alleys. *Shellum Bowling Hall of Fame collection*

mouth of the Hudson River from the local Indians for approximately $24 worth of beads and cloth. After building Fort Amsterdam in the new settlement, Minuit quickly lay the grounds for a bowling green on the southern tip of the island. The thin pins were set up in a diamond pattern and victory went to the first bowler to topple exactly 31 pins. If the slightly taller central "kingpin" fell over first, the bowler automatically won.

When Old New York was still New Amsterdam, the Dutch passed what was probably America's first bowling ban. To protect the holy day of rest, laws prohibited two pleasurable acts on Sundays: bowling and picking strawberries. Perhaps early addicts of bowling could evade this law by crossing the river to the other Dutch settlement of Breuckelen (today's Brooklyn).

In 1664, King Charles II of England grew envious of this Dutch paradise. The jealous king wrote up a charter that gave his brother James, the Duke of York, all of New Netherland, including America's first bowling green. When faced with British warships, the Dutch colonists capitulated and gave up their beloved bowling lawn. The victors quickly rewrote bowling history to give the earlier explorer Henry Hudson—an Englishman—credit for introducing nine-pin skittle bowling to New York. Bowling Green still lies in Battery Park near Wall Street and is surrounded by towering skyscrapers.

Like other settlers to the New World, William Penn (after whom Pennsylvania is named) fell under bowling's spell and spent hours rolling the ball. After being criticized for bowing to the game's temptation and neglecting his governing duties, Penn justified his time at the lanes in a 1673 letter: "At my time the bowls themselves furnish a seemly and good diversion."

Meanwhile, in New England, Puritans struggled to ebb the influence of knocking down skittles. As Satan tempted

READY TO ROLL Early bowling attire varied little from office clothes: skinny tie, button-down shirt, and flood pants. *Shellum Bowling Hall of Fame collection*

LEE ROY JOHNS "He did not take up bowling, except in a desultory way, until 1900," reads the back of this Mecca Cigarettes bowling trading card. After two perfect games in match tournaments, Lee Roy Johns bought a bowling alley in Newark. *Shellum Bowling Hall of Fame collection*

DUNBAR THE GREAT With an average of just 206, Dunbar was the national champion bowler from 1908 to 1910. Mecca Cigarettes ran this series of champion bowlers trading cards as an added bonus to its Virginia tobacco. *Shellum Bowling Hall of Fame collection*

WAIT UNTIL THE PINBOY HAS FINISHED! Dropping down in the pit to steady the pins, these adolescent pinboys pose for a photo in 1909 at the Arcade Bowling Alley in Trenton, New Jersey. Notice the duck pins in lanes 5 and 6.

23

Millburn Recreation Bowling Academy

MORRIS TURNPIKE AND FARLEY PLACE, MILLBURN, N.J.

BOWLING AND ALSO AN OLD ENGLISH TAP ROOM

AMPLE PARKING SPACE

Peter J. Farley, Prop.
Millburn 6-1859

young girls in Salem, Massachusetts, and 19 witches were hanged for collaborating with demons, bans were also placed on "dice, cards, quoits, bowls, ninepins, 'or any other unlawful game in house, yard, garden or backside...in howses of Common Interteinment, whereby much precious time is spent unfruitfully,'" according to Foster Dulles in *America Learns to Play*.

Before he became president, John Adams wrote that his native Massachusetts was a breeding ground for vice in spite of these laws outlawing games. In 1761, he described a visit to a New England tavern and a clandestine skittle alley: "If you sit the evening, you will find the house full of people, drinking, drams, flip, toddy, carousing, swearing." Bowling was considered as sinful as cock fighting, drunkenness, and soliciting strumpets.

Nearly 60 years later, in 1819, author Washington Irving claimed the mighty mantle of the first American writer to mention bowling in his work. In his tale of a Dutch sleepyhead snoozing in the Catskills, he described "a company of odd-looking personages playing at nine-pins...the noise of the balls echoed along the mountains like rumbling peals of thunder."

OLD ENGLISH ALLEY In an attempt to preserve ye olde English manor feel of the Henry the VIII days, the Millburn Recreation Bowling Academy kept its grounds well manicured and advertised the "Old English Tap Room." *Shellum Bowling Hall of Fame collection*

V FOR VICTORY This early matchbook cover from California was probably made right after World War I and named in honor of the victory of the Great War. *Shellum Bowling Hall of Fame collection*

In spite of a noteworthy appearance in the nation's blossoming literature, colonists still viewed bowling as a corruptive influence among the men of America. The Connecticut legislature passed an act forbidding nine-pin lanes in that state and attached severe consequences to any infraction. A bowling legend claims that resourceful rollers simply added a tenth pin and set them up in a diamond pattern. Since the games of nine- and ten-pin were similar enough to each other, bowlers didn't mind switching to avoid a run-in with Officer Friendly. With ten-pin bowling—whose likely origin seems to stem from Britain or Holland—legal in any state, alleys soon filled the new cities from coast to coast. This was the birth of bowling American-style.

MILADY BOWLING Before stylish bowling outfits were sewn for female keglers, ladies wore their evening gowns and managed to hold their own in high heels.

UP YOUR ALLEY While women were often encouraged to bowl, chubby female (and male) bowlers were spoofed in joke cards. *Shellum Bowling Hall of Fame collection*

Most areas—from Polynesia to Paris—have their own variation of bowling. Pins come in various shapes, from pyramids to ducks, and candlesticks to obelisks. Some forms, like lawn bowling, don't even use pins. Apart from games with names like goriziana, halfboard, quilles (a.k.a., *kayless, cayles,* and *keiles*), basque, boccette, platzbahkegln, and others too numerous to name, here are some of the most popular variations on bowling:

Duck pins—The short, wide pins wobble like ducks before falling. The balls are only 5 inches in diameter and the pins are about 9 1/2 inches tall. The legend goes that Baltimore natives Wilbert Robinson and John McGraw carved broken pins into squat duck pins in 1898 to invent a new form of bowling with three balls in a frame. The story falls apart, though, when records show a duck pin tournament played in 1894 in Massachusetts, four years earlier.

Candlepins—This variation on regular ten-pin bowling began when a 17-year-old wanted to create an easier game. Or at least that's how the story goes. The 10 candlestick pins are slender cylinders measuring 15 3/4 inches high and bowing out a bit in the middle. The ball is only 4 1/2 inches in diameter and three balls can be rolled in a frame. Along with duck pins, candlepins are played mostly on the eastern seaboard of the United States and Canada.

Bocce—Known as "petanque" in France or "lawn bowling" in England, bocce is usually played outside on a clay alley, although sometimes it is played on grass, dirt, or ground gravel. A small ball called a "jack" is thrown and the bowlers launch their balls in an attempt to be the closest to the little red jack.

Nine-pins—The pins are set up in the shape of a diamond and a taller "kingpin" stands in the middle. Played mostly in northern Europe, nine-pins has variations called "nine-pin skittles," "clossynge," and "closh."

Five-pins—Often called "Canadian Five Pins," this game has 10 frames and the bowler can roll three times in each, unless a strike or spare is scored. The small ball is 5 inches in diameter. A spare or strike counts for 15 points.

Curling—Played on an ice rink, curling was developed either in Scotland or Holland, depending on the source. During a "bonspiel," or tournament, the curler slides an enormous stone with a handle from the "hack," or foothold, down the sheet toward the "house," or target. If the "skip," or captain, wants the stone to go farther, he or she will yell "sweep!" Two teammates jump on the ice with brooms and sweep in front of the stone. Curling has been an official Olympic sport since 1998.

Shuffleboard—Perhaps a bit of a stretch from bowling, shuffleboard (originally called "shovelboard") involves pushing disks with a "cue" on to a numbered target. English royalty played shuffleboard along with lawn bowling at least as far back as the 1400s.

Chapter Two

BOWLING ALLEYS

Medieval bowling alleys consisted of packed-down clay, dirt, ashes, perfectly flat slate, or foot-and-a-half-wide wooden planks. While the British, Dutch, French, and Italians often preferred lawn bowling on a sunny day, the Swiss rolled their balls down a board in a game called *platzbahkegln*.

Saloons expanded with bowling lanes to lure in customers to roll a few lines and drink a few rounds. America's first indoor lane was probably Knickerbocker Alleys in Manhattan, which dates back to 1840. All the wealthy robber barons—the Vanderbilts, Astors, and Roosevelts—dressed to the nines to bowl on the baked-clay lanes of this sleek new alley.

Soon, Times Square was packed with bowling alleys and the sensation spread across the country. The influx of German and Polish immigrants brought their love of bowling with them as they settled ever farther west. Soon, the German term *kegler* became synonymous with *bowler* in Midwestern alleys.

In an attempt to lure patrons and keep clientele, "Billiards and Bowling" signs hung from many saloons. In Chicago, "More than one out of eight [pool/billiard] rooms had either liquor licenses or bowling alleys in order to compete," according to Steven Reiss in *City Games*. Barkeeps persuaded the regulars to stay for more beer or booze by giving away free games.

To promote their lanes, colorful matchbooks were given out. Two- and three-color printing on matchbooks featured cheesecake paintings of seductive girlies awkwardly bowling with a flash of underwear and punning captions like "striking," "sit-down strike," or "what a frame!" While waiting for your

FIRST ABC With a long lineage of bowling, Mort Luby has taken his passion of bowling from the lanes to the canvas. Luby's grandfather began the *Bowlers Journal*, the oldest monthly sports journal in America, and Mort grew up around the alley. Now Mort Luby paints from his studio in Carpentersville, Illinois. Here he portrays the first ABC competition held in Chicago in 1901. *Mort Luby*

turn to bowl, what better way to pass the time than sipping a beer, smoking a cig, and checking out the gal on your matchbook cover?

Not everyone was excited about bowling saloons. On December 15, 1855, a group of women in Lincoln, Illinois, had had enough. Fed up with the debauchery of these halls of sin, these puritanical ladies attacked Boyd's Bowling Saloon armed with axes, hatchets, shovels, and knives. When their demands that the alley close shop weren't followed, the angry teetotalers torched the tobacco, smashed the supplies of liquor, and nearly burnt the building to the ground. Alley owners got the message. Some bowling centers opened their doors to women and children. That same year in Milwaukee, Mr. Burns encouraged women to bowl and form leagues. Signs were posted along the lanes that advised men not to curse in the presence of the ladies. Alley employees were beseeched to shave at least twice daily. While smoking stayed, the spittoons were removed.

Lanes varied wildly in the 1850s. The length and width of the alleys weren't standardized, nor was the size or shape of pins. The balls formed grooves down the center of the wooden lanes, so rolling a strike was a cinch. Clumping the pins close to each other ensured more perfect games and more happy customers. With the Civil War looming, however, agreeing on bowling regulations had to wait.

Finally, in 1875, a group of nine New York bowling clubs gathered to form the National Bowling Association. Pin dimensions were standardized and the distance from the foul line to the pins could be no less than 60 feet. Still, outsiders questioned the authority of the Big Apple bowling clubs. In 1890, the American Bowling League was founded, but it didn't stay together. Finally, on September 9, 1895, Joe Thum, "The Father of Bowling," founded the ABC (American Bowling Congress) at Beethoven Hall in New York after negotiating with many other bowling clubs. The New Yorkers could no longer play by their own rules, and national bowling competitions could now be launched at any alley that fit the standards.

Consequently, 1895 was the year ten-pin bowling became an acceptable sport to the general public in the United States. The March 1937 issue of *The Literary Digest*

This early black-and-white photo shows the care taken to achieve perfectly level lanes and sleek surfaces in the new standardized lanes.
Shellum Bowling Hall of Fame collection

A Sure Strike

Pin Cushion

deckard

SIT DOWN STRIKE

CALENDAR GIRLS These buxom babes were plastered across early calendars for bowling alleys and the occasional service station. What guy wouldn't want women like this to spice up their league night? Bowling center owners often borrowed these paintings for matchbook covers to advertise their alleys. When real female bowlers showed up at the lanes, though, men sometimes teased them about their bowling skills and made cat calls—at least until the women out-scored them. *Shellum Bowling Hall of Fame collection*

BEER-N-BOWL Schmidt Brewing Company sent alleys this bowling display that measured more than 6 feet long. If "Everybody likes a winner," read the ad with the hidden subtext, "Nobody Likes a Loser. *Shellum Bowling Hall of Fame collection*

BEER TEAM When Prohibition was repealed, breweries were ready to bring back the beer to bowling. Some alley owners were hesitant because they worked hard to create a family atmosphere during the dry years. Breweries formed beer teams to tour alleys, and most alleys soon let the beer flow. *Shellum Bowling Hall of Fame collection*

BRING ON THE BEER! After Prohibition, when alley owners were worried about reintroducing beer into the family-friendly atmosphere, Schlitz and other breweries mounted bowling campaigns to prove that beer can bring couples together. After World War II, men and women bowled together as shown on the scorecard of this 1957 ad. Big breweries also pushed beer back into the bowling alleys by pointing out to owners that they could double their profits on league night. According to *Bowling Alone*, "...league bowlers consume three times as much beer and pizza as do solo bowlers, and the money in bowling is in the beer and pizza, not the balls and shoes." Notice the hand towel in the background—this 1947 Pabst ad predates Brunswick's 1956 "Electric-Aire Hand Dryer." *Shellum Bowling Hall of Fame collection*

wrote, "Before 1895, bowling was pretty much of a hoodlum sport. Cheap gamblers and bar-room bruisers had just about ruined the game....Even the alleys were crooked. Rolling a perfect score down a time-worn groove was simple."

Early alleys were entertainment complexes with a café, restaurant, and dance hall on the ground floor, perhaps billiards and pool on the second, and bowling on the top floor. While bowling halls welcomed women, the dim lights of the dark alleys clouded by smoke caused most women to venture inside only when accompanied by a date.

Banning Beer

In 1910, alleys were in a slump because the cost to set up a bowling alley scared bar owners, so they opted to run pool halls instead. In Chicago alone, nearly 40 percent of

Here's how... Connie Schwoegler rolls a Smooth strike

1. **Smooth New "Fingertip-grip"** is an innovation of Connie Schwoegler's ball, fingers fit only to the first joint. The wider span of the hand with this ball makes it easier to control, easier to send it hooking smoothly into the one-three pocket for a strike or for those all-important spares.

2. **Smooth Footwork** is a secret of Schwoegler's graceful 5-step delivery. Here, in his fourth step, he starts downswing, begins to impart a smooth turn to the ball. Smooth, by the way, is the word for Hamm's Beer. Hamm's smooth and mellow flavor has made it first choice of millions of highly discriminating beer drinkers for 84 years.

3. **Smooth Delivery!** Schwoegler applies hook by rolling hand over top of ball, thumb acting as pivot while fingers do the work. A bowler's bowler, he's rolled eight perfect 300 games. A connoisseur's beer, Hamm's gives perfect pleasure in those mellow moments when only the best is good enough. Hamm's is made for mellow moments.

4. **"Here's How!" for Mellow Moments:** Whether you roll 300 or 120, a foaming glass of Hamm's Beer makes it a perfect game. Hamm's is smooth and mellow—the beer for mellow moments when all's right with the world. But words can't tell you how smooth and mellow Hamm's Beer tastes. You have to try Hamm's to find out what you've been missing. Now, plant expansion makes this old favorite of millions more widely available, so try Hamm's. Take just one taste, a *single taste!* For mellow moments, "Here's How!" with Hamm's Beer.

Here's how...with
Hamm's Beer
Smooth and Mellow

THEO. HAMM BREWING CO.
ST. PAUL, MINN.

SMOOTH STRIKE, SMOOTH BEER Instructing bowlers on the perfect form, Connie Schwoegler and Hamm's slip in some drinking tips. "Whether you roll 300 or 120, a foaming glass of Hamm's Beer makes it a perfect game." *Bob Dzandzara collection*

alleys closed from 1910 to 1918, perhaps due in part to World War I.

When the Great War came to a close, bowling alley owners braced for the next big slump: Prohibition. Surprisingly, bowling alleys boomed during this time. In 1920, the newly formed ABC sanctioned 450 alleys in the United States, and 2,000 were sanctioned by the end of the decade. According to *City Games,* Chicago saw a 41 percent increase in bowling alleys in 1919, and

"Bowling began to lose its connection with the low-life sporting fraternity and came to be regarded as a source of good clean fun."

To better the standards of bowling, the Bowling Proprietors' Association of America was formed in 1932. Few alley owners could risk the penalty of a speakeasy in the basement or selling bathtub gin behind the bar. Instead, bowling was sold as wholesome family recreation. More lights, new curtains, fresh paint, and less smoking all contributed to a family-friendly atmosphere at the new "dry alleys."

In 1933 when ads declared that "Beer is Back!" breweries assumed that alleys would revert to the pre-Prohibition days of suds on tap. Bowling alleys were faced with a dilemma of whether to cave in or keep the alcohol-free family atmosphere. Brewers created the famous "Beer Teams" to promote both bowling and beer. Only men's teams toured, while breweries failed to recognize the expanding number of female keglers. Stroh's Falstaff, Meister Brau, Pabst Blue Ribbon, Hamm's, Blatz, Pfeiffer's, and Gluek's all had their team of ringers in color-coordinated outfits. Little by little, beer made its way back into most alleys as a cure for the symptoms of the Great Depression.

Bowling for Victory

The 1940s were bowling's boom years. There were slumps in bowling during the Civil War and World War I, but the newly formed bowling associations pushed bowling as a patriotic sport—never mind that Nazi keglers loved to bowl too. Bowling stars toured military bases "to lecture, instruct, and give exhibitions [to] service people." Walter Cleveland, bowler extraordinaire, toured 263 service camps to give demonstrations.

With the young men overseas, the Rosie the Riveters working in the factories spent their leisure time at the lanes. Because factories ran night and day, league bowling was scheduled for all hours and after any shift. Bowling alleys flourished during this time.

V FOR VICTORY Since bowling was the preferred sport of female factory workers, wartime propaganda posters used the ball and pins motif to encourage overtime to smash those fascists.

NAZI KEGLERS Bowling was the patriotic sport for American GIs and their honeys back home. Little did they know that the Jerries were bowling in Berlin, as shown in this wartime postcard.

To supply recreational equipment to the troops, a "Bowlers Victory Legion" was created in 1942. An old Bowlers Victory League ad in the form of a letter from a GI encouraged bowlers to chip in by saying that "each piece [is] marked 'from the Bowlers of America' Bowlers, do your share. I'll do mine over here. Thanks, Your Buddy Johnny Brown."

To help support the troops overseas, both the USO and the Red Cross set up fundraisers at bowling alleys. A National War Bond Bowling Tournament sponsored a "Bowlers Victory League" to raise money for American troops. The Women's International Bowling Congress (WIBC), founded in 1916, began a "Buy a Bomber" and "Wings of Mercy" programs and raised a staggering $500,000. The once-dainty lady bowlers gave the Air Force a Douglas A-20 attack bomber that was named *Miss WIBC*. The Wings of Mercy program bought three hospital planes named *Miss Nightingale I, II,* and *III*. With more Allied bowlers than Axis keglers, Hitler's storm troopers didn't have a chance.

Immediately after the war, "in occupied Germany alone, the American GIs formed 500 leagues," according to *The Big Book of Bowling*. Bowling alley owners and leagues convinced businesses who had supported the troops to now sponsor a team. Finally, men and the women who waited for them could bowl together at the local lanes. Gambling was out, but high-stakes contests were in for both sexes.

In 1920 America had 1,450 alleys, but the number blossomed to 6,097 by 1949. According to the book *City Games*, however, "[Bowling alleys in the 1930s] were also kept out of middle-class peripheral neighborhoods by zoning laws." After the war, bowling slowly became an accepted family pastime. In Chicago, 62 percent more alleys appeared between 1945 and 1955. Bowling was about to enter its golden age.

Pinboys' Last Stand

One of the biggest obstacles for bowling alleys was keeping pinboys in line. Perched on the ledge until the bowler's ball knocked over the pins, the pinboy then jumped down into the pit and cleared the fallen pins. Some advanced alleys had a metal or wooden frame in which to arrange the pins and lower them

Bowling Alleys.
Moncton Victoria Club, Moncton N.B.

DECORATIVE PINBOYS This hand-colored postcard features an early Canadian alley in New Brunswick with the pinboys on semi-permanent display at the end of the lanes.

perfectly into place. Otherwise, the grueling task of standing each pin up thousands of times a day fell on the pinboy. This dead-end job to set up pins almost endlessly was often filled by imbibing dropouts who couldn't find other work. Impatient bowlers taunted pinboys to hurry up, and pinboys harassed bad bowlers. Pinboys jeered and leered at women bowlers, and many women stayed away from bowling because of the teasing.

Nevertheless, pinboys were the workhorses of bowling. Professor and former pinboy Charlie Sugnet recalls, "We would sit above the pit and if a ball was thrown exceptionally hard, we risked being hit by a wayward pin. Then we'd hop down on the lane and set 'em up on the little markers. We weren't paid by the hour, but by the game."

When the 1937 ABC Tournament met in New York "the 45 pinboys will have to pick up approximately 47,300,000 pounds of pins during the tournament. Pinboys get $5 a day for working in the Congress, and must have had 10 years' experience to qualify," according to *The Literary Digest* from March 1937. Right after the war, a pinboy union was formed in New York City and had 5,000 members. Pinboys ran up the alley's overhead to cut down on owners' profits, and many of the young workers had to be home soon after dark.

When Robert E. Kennedy witnessed a crude pin-setting machine in 1936, he knew pinboys would be passé very soon. Gottfried Schmidt invented the first contraption and the American Machine and Foundry

PINBOYS' NEMESIS Pinboys no longer had to risk being struck by an errant pin, but they also couldn't collect their pittance for each game played. After AMF introduced the automatic pinsetting machine, Brunswick soon took AMF to task with its own version.

Company (AMF) purchased the patent for the first prototype in 1946, which was fraught with foibles. Coming from the "bakery, tobacco, and apparel businesses," AMF jumped into bowling before it built golf carts and owned Harley-Davidson. Finally, in August 1951, the world's first functioning pinsetting machine was installed in the Bowl-O-Drome in Mount Clemens, Michigan. Voyeurs from far and wide came to witness this mechanical marvel and bowl at one of the 12 automatic lanes. In 1952, Farragut Pool Lanes in Brooklyn worked out the quirks of the robotic pinsetters for its 16 fully automatic lanes.

"AMF put me out of my first job!" recalls Sugnet. Many alleys stayed open 24 hours because pinboys were now obsolete.

From Alley to Center

Now that owners didn't need to pull urchins off the streets to set up pins, bowling alleys spread to the suburbs. Automatic pinsetting machines weren't the only contraption to propel bowling into the jet age, however. AMF's competitor Brunswick invented the first "Electric-Aire Hand Dryer" in 1956 to keep a bowler's sweaty hand from slipping out of the holes. The chalk used to dry a bowler's hand was outdated, and the grubby rag dangling by the balls could be retired. Bad bowlers could no longer weep into this "crying towel" when missing a 7-10 split.

Air conditioning allowed alleys to open their doors all summer long, and bowlers couldn't blame the heat for a bad frame. In fact, people sought out the alley to cool down on scorching hot days.

To keep score, old slate boards with dusty chalk were tossed out in favor of slick desks with an angled top for keeping track of strikes and spares. Ultramodern lanes had glass scorecards with a light shining through to project on the screen above.

Booths made of molded plastic and covered with glittery Naugahyde proved that bowling had moved from the barroom to art deco masterpieces. In the old alleys, the spectators watched on clunky wooden stools. New alleys with curvilinear booths were designed to create a social atmosphere. In *System of Objects,* cultural theorist Jean Baudrillard reasoned that:

"Modern seating...invariably lays the stress on sociability and conversation, promoting a sort of all-purpose position, appropriate to the modern social human being, which de-emphasizes everything in the sitting posture that suggests confrontation...one no longer sits opposite anyone. It is impossible to become angry in such seats, or to argue, or to seek to persuade. They dictate a relaxed social interaction which makes no demands, which is open-ended but above all open to play...Seats of this kind may well respond to...the

Continued on page 43

The beautiful Bryant-Lake Bowl waitresses lure in customers from Lake Street in Minneapolis, Minnesota, to the most unusual alley in the Midwest. For years, the alley was in a tough part of town and the lanes were never updated. When the Bryant-Lake Bowl changed hands, only Roger, who has tended the lanes for decades, stayed on. The aged lanes with the open ball return were now considered a time capsule of classic bowling alleys. The large videogame room was transformed into an avant-garde theater with such bizarre performances as a goofy adrenaline-filled theatrical version of the surfer flick *Point Break*; screenings of *Mary Tyler Marx*, a redubbed 1970s sitcom with revolutionary gags; and screaming feedback guitar solos by the female lead singer of the band Jan who rolled around naked in Fruit Loops, Crisco, and an oversized salami. Hollywood has discovered this little gem of an alley, and Matt Dillon and Uma Thurman stopped in to film a portion of the blockbuster *Beautiful Girls* here. Waiter John Perkins, who sometimes performs on stage as an inebriated Buddhist monk with a freshly shaven head, sums up the unusual clientele, "The Bryant-Lake Bowl is a big lesbian hangout...and I love it!"

LITTLE ALLEY ON THE PRARIE To bowl a few lines in Edgeley, North Dakota, just call ahead and they'll open it up. Make sure you remember to turn off the lights and lock the door on your way out.

WORLD'S SMALLEST BOWLING ALLEY? Just east of Mobridge in the tiny town of Selby, South Dakota, lies what some have called the World's Smallest Bowling Alley. The competition to this dubious title was in Lawrence Welk's hometown of Strasburg, North Dakota, but the latter two-laned alley burned to the ground. Some of the Champagne-Music North Dakotans suspected their envious neighbors to the south were responsible for the fire, but so far no border war has erupted.

FAIR CITY LANES Huron, South Dakota, boasts the "World's Largest Pheasant," which is perched on top of a building on the highway. Because of this stiff competition for attention, Fair City Lanes had to mount a sleek sign on the roof to draw in bowlers mesmerized by the big bird.

THE STARDUST Named for the Las Vegas casino and the Hoagy Carmichael song, the Stardust Lanes are located in Minneapolis' "Hub of Hell," named for all the railroad tracks that converge nearby. Local mock rock trio Vinnie and the Stardusters named themselves after a drunk mafioso who was kicked out of the Stardust, a family establishment that hosts grade-school children during the day.

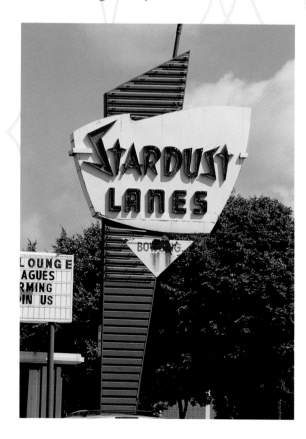

LOOK FOR THE TRIANGLE Why not Minot? Just south of the enormous Minot Air Force Base in North Dakota, this bowling alley seeks to distract the airmen from their duties manning the intercontinental ballistic missiles to try their luck at the lanes.

LITHO POSTCARD This lithographed card hails from the home of Mayo Clinic, so no wonder the back of the card advocates how the sport gives bowlers "a new feeling of 'aliveness.' " The fancy "York Air Conditioning" installed at the Dunlap allowed people to bowl "no matter what the outside temperature may be."

300 BOWL In the sweaty heat of Phoenix, Arizona, the 300 Bowl boasted it was "refrigerated and heat conditioned for perfect comfort." With wild cantilever roofs that echoed Cadillac tail fins, the ultramodern design could inspire any bowler to roll a perfect game.

Continued from page 38

wish never to be alone—but never to be face to face with another person either."

While the bistros of Paris, the pubs of London, or the cafés of Vienna bred revolutionaries in search of the perfect society, the bowling alleys of America spawned a nation in search of the perfect game. Many new alleys opened alongside train tracks so workers could roll a few lines after working on the railroad. During tough times, empty alleys could be converted into warehouses. Most new alleys opened in new suburban shopping centers to nab mom on her shopping trip. Living in tract housing called for a weekend trip to the sparkly new strip mall to bowl and one never had to leave suburbia.

Bowling books professed that alleys bring bosses and employees together in a neutral, fun atmosphere to socialize away from the tension of the office or factory. Ads of the time showed that since both husband and wife bowled, they shared a common activity and supposedly became closer. Bowling alleys had become the new gathering place for families in the suburbs.

To lure families into the new bowling entertainment complex, alley owners stole the styling cue of lavish marquees from movie theaters. Some alleys, such as McCook Bowl in Dayton, Ohio, featured an architectural marvel of 44 consecutive lanes with no posts blocking the view.

Amidst the shag carpeting and Streamline Moderne, cocktail lounges replaced the smoky bars of yore. Exotic themes and modernist architecture boasted a worldly experience with fruity highballs before bowling a line. The Aztec Room, Inca Room, Totem Lounge, and Kona Kove promised a journey to pre-Conquest kitsch. Blast off to outer space in the Starlite Room (with stylized comets exploding in print), the Planet Room (with a planetarium-styled

STYLISH SIGNAGE To compete with motels, bowling alleys had brightly lit space-age signs to lure prospective bowlers to pull over the Ford and bowl. *Shellum Bowling Hall of Fame collection*

BIZARRE BOWLING ARCHITECTURE From A-Frames to shells to dining car diners to cantilever roofs, bowling alley architecture freely borrowed all the best Americana styles. *Shellum Bowling Hall of Fame collection*

BOWLING MARQUEES Stealing a styling cue from movie theaters, bowling alleys near Tinseltown attracted the vacationers bored with the latest Clark Gable talkie. *Shellum Bowling Hall of Fame collection*

roof), the Neptune Room (with the star-studded god bearing his trident), or the Orbit Room at Mercury Bowl (with drawings of atoms waiting to be split). This was a new era unafraid to explore other cultures in the safety of its cocktail lounge.

In 1959, *The Woman's Bowling Guide* expounded on these spectacular alleys: "Bowling establishments of a half century ago...were confined mostly to evil-smelling basements and they spawned cutthroat gambling. Today they are recreational fairylands where your young daughters may bowl in a clean, spacious atmosphere of complete safety."

Life magazine ran a large feature in the 1950s and praised these new bowling centers with their "deep-carpeted lobbies." In an article called "A New Luxury World of Bowling," *Life* applauded by saying, "The American bowling alley, once stuck shamefacedly in a back-street basement, has acquired a stunning elegance and has bloomed into an all-purpose

pleasure palace...and...its façades have the glitter of a Hollywood nightclub."

Life corrects itself, however, by pointing out "...only they are not called alleys anymore. They are more delicately known as lanes." Juette Holseth, editor of *Metro Bowler*, is quick to correct anyone making *Life*'s mistake. "They're called 'bowling centers,' not 'alleys,'" she advises, since "lane" can be synonymous with "alley." Some even prefer the more neutral "bowling establishment" or "bowling house." This apparently docile discussion about the correct word has erupted into a semantic argument. To put the fight to rest, a 2005 survey on bowl.com found that 60 percent of bowlers still call it an "alley," not a "center."

Regardless, bowling has boomed from the little two-lane centers in any small town in the United States to the world's largest bowling complex in Tokyo, Japan. This enormous alley towers seven stories into the air and every day 10,000 to 30,000 bowlers fill the 252 lanes.

LOUNGE HAVEN

LOUNGE HEAVEN The cocktail lounge was just as important for customers as offering a nursery for babies or air conditioning. Going to the bowling alley was no longer a smoky dismal affair. Instead, classy alleys offered the latest lounges with everything from the Gay Nineties Lounge to the Magic Carpet Room. Or, as one matchbook advised before bowling, "Cocktails in the Pin Room, Dine in the Lotus Room." *Shellum Bowling Hall of Fame collection*

FROM GERMAN U-BOATS TO BOWLING

When the Nazis stormed into Norway, thanks to the traitorous Vidkun Quisling, the fjords were deemed perfect ports for the German navy. The deep-water inlets protected by towering mountains made it difficult for enemy bombers or other ships to surprise the Nazi fleet.

The Germans used Trondheim, the third-largest city in Norway, as a base to build its *Unterseeboote,* or U-boats. An enormous factory named DORA-1 with cement walls 5 meters thick was raised on the pier next to the fjord. Allied bombers couldn't

destroy the enormous structure as the Germans pumped out these submarines to sink thousands of merchant ships. The Axis' 13th Flotilla based in Trondheim was the scourge of the North Atlantic. Even by the time the Germans surrendered in May 1945, the DORA-1 factory lay intact and had produced 55 U-boats during the war.

The Norwegians sought to destroy this enormous concrete reminder of Nazi occupation at the end of the pier. The cement was too thick to budge even with dynamite. Rather than waste time and money deconstructing DORA-1, the local government resolved to turn this eyesore into entertainment. Along with storage for the local museum, a bowling alley was opened in part of DORA-1 for the local shiphands to unwind by rolling a line after unloading cargo or spending weeks at sea.

CHICAGO

19

ABC GOLDEN ANNIVERSARY CHAMPIONSHIPS

AMERICAN BOWLING CONGRESS

Chapter Three

A SOCIAL SPORT

Beer-and-Pretzel vs. Coffee-and-Doughnut Leagues

In the 1890s, dreams of a bowling league to rival baseball's National League filled the minds of high-scoring keglers. The National Bowling League was created to feature "at the lanes entertainment with singers, dancers, clowns, and chimpanzees that bowled." The New York Gladiators bowling team projected a "40-lane center magically suspended over the main waiting room in New York City's Grand Central Station." The National Bowling League was put to rest when the Detroit Thunderbirds soundly slaughtered the Twin City Skippers in three straight matches.

In 1895, the *Bowlers Journal* sponsored a tournament with eight of the best professional bowling teams. Within two years, this new club went belly-up. Joe Thum, a German immigrant who was lovingly dubbed the "Father of Bowling," tried his best by organizing the United Bowling Clubs (UBC). Once again, the club didn't last, even with the White Elephant, his fancy new alley with luxurious electric lights.

Only after the famous meeting at Beethoven Hall in New York City in 1895 and 1896, could the newly formed American Bowling Congress (ABC) provide the legitimacy for a true national tournament. In 1901, the first ABC competition was held in Chicago and became an annual event that has lasted for more than a century.

With a bona fide bowling league to rival baseball, bowlers began founding minor-league clubs across the country. At the time Al Capone was stuffed in the pen for tax evasion, 500,000 Chicagoans claimed the title of "bowler" and filled the local lanes with 900 leagues. A third of the proprietors were born abroad, primarily Germans, and the majority of bowlers were new immigrants.

1953 ABC Bowling leagues from across the country gathered in the Windy City for the biggest annual tournament of them all. A different stand that listed the city with a slick bowling logo was built each year for team photos. *Shellum Bowling Hall of Fame collection*

Weekends were made for bowling and beer. When not at the drive-in theater, couples would throw strikes and spares with their friends while munching on a burger. From the German influence, men formed "beer-and-pretzel leagues" as women followed with "coffee-and-doughnut leagues" with nurseries to watch the kids. "Bowling houses" split from shady pool halls and within a generation were considered acceptable places for ladies of repute.

Early alleys even opened their doors to handicapped bowlers. At the 1937 ABC tournament in New York, Carl Rice, a blind bowler, rolled a score of 196 (down from his high of 257). According to *The Literary Digest* from 1937, "Rice has a super-developed sense of hearing that almost compensates for his lack of sight. Usually he can tell what pins are standing after the crash." Later articles on handicapped bowlers weren't so kind. In March 1959, *Bowling Magazine* titled an article about a group of Arizonan men in wheelchairs or on crutches: "Lame Ducks Have Fun in Tucson."

The second-biggest new market for bowling—after women—was youngsters. The title of the "Father of Bowling" had already been nabbed by Joe Thum, but Chicago high school teacher Milton Raymer claimed the coveted title of the "Father of Junior Bowling." In 1936,

junior leagues began bowling, and by 1946 the American High School Bowling Congress boasted 8,767 members. Today, this youth association has half a million members and is known as the YABA, or Young American Bowling Alliance.

Once a den of sin and vice, bowling alleys were deemed "family-friendly." Kids begged their parents to let them celebrate their birthday parties at the local alley—an idea unimaginable before World War II. Teenagers had long ago discovered bowling's allure, however. In *City Games,* Steven Reiss points out:

"Bowling also facilitated sociability with the opposite sex. Alleys provided a public, nonthreatening environment where street-corner boys could meet groups of young women and enjoy their companionship without the awkwardness that often accompanied blind dates....Young Italian South Bostonians... in the late 1930s talked about bowling more than any other topic. Each fellow's status in the group was correlated with his bowling prowess."

To be a professional bowler was to be complete. "Far more compelling than the money or the diamond-studded gold medals for first place is the distinction of being, for a year, the ABC champion," according to *The Literary Digest* in 1937. To be a winner didn't mean muscle building, following a strict dietary regimen, or to give up imbibing or smoking. To become a champion meant simply to bowl as much as possible. Bowling carried the dubious distinction of being a sport that required skill but not necessarily physical fitness. Bowling is the everyman's and everywoman's sport.

The Professional Bowlers Association (PBA) and the Professional Women's Bowling Association

OFFICIAL SCHEDULE
1933 SILVER ANNIVERSARY 1933

Recreation Alleys

Minneapolis Recreation Building
714 Hennepin Ave.
MINNEAPOLIS, MINN.

FEBRUARY
11th to 19th
Inclusive
1933

TWENTY-FIFTH ANNUAL TOURNAMENT
Sanctioned by the American Bowling Congress
INTERNATIONAL BOWLING ASSOCIATION

TOURNAMENT PROGRAM When the International Bowling Association met in Minneapolis in 1933, this sleek, shiny schedule was passed around for the silver anniversary. *Shellum Bowling Hall of Fame collection*

SIPPING SODA Following another victory on the lanes, the boys partake in a drink in this air-brushed glossy. *Shellum Bowling Hall of Fame collection*

ABC CHAMPS Besides the usual team snapshot behind the podium or on the lanes, these champs march by the ABC for a photo op. *Shellum Bowling Hall of Fame collection*

ALL HAIL THE KING! Following the tournament, the queen crowns the new champion, who dons a royal robe of satin. *Shellum Bowling Hall of Fame collection*

(PWBA) were formed in 1959. Another ill-fated National Bowling League—similar to the one from the nineteenth century—was dreamed up in 1961. A big bowling scandal was unveiled before the first ball was even rolled as rivals claimed one of their ilk tried to bribe Don Carter with promises of a pig farm. The NBL died a swift death as most bowlers hesitated to give up their status as part of the Professional Bowlers Association to join.

In spite of bowling's position as the most-played sport in the world, international respect has eluded the humble sport. Even though bowling was introduced at the 1936 Olympics and Hank Marino from the United States easily won all events, the Olympic Committee has balked at declaring bowling a sanctioned Olympic sport.

All Bowlers Are Created Equal

African American track star Jesse Owens threw a figurative pie in Adolf Hitler's face in 1936. The Führer's theory of Aryan supremacy fell flat when Owens ran away with four gold medals at the 1936 Berlin Olympics. Bowling was introduced at the same Olympics, but the ABC ignored the lesson learned. African Americans were unable to become members in the ABC or bowl in its tournament.

In earlier times, when bowling was relegated to saloons, racial criteria weren't generally enforced at alleys. In fact, ABC's first president, Thomas Curtis, didn't perceive bowling to be an exclusive sport in 1895 and wanted to include all races and both genders. Curtis was far too liberal in his bowling views and was silenced by the majority of the ABC. In 1915, the ABC declared that all members must be of the "white male sex."

Black bowlers could not be kept down and founded the National Negro Bowling Association (NNBA) on August 20, 1939, at the Frogs Club in Detroit. Just like baseball's Negro Leagues, the African American bowling league ran its own clubs and tournaments.

Racism didn't strike only African Americans. In 1943, Japanese American bowling champ Fuzzy Shimada was scooped up from a bowling alley where he worked as a

1978 CHAMPS The 1970s hairdos complement that era's logos when the ABC met under the St. Louis, Missouri, arch. Six years later, the International Bowling Hall of Fame moved from Milwaukee, Wisconsin, to St. Louis. *Shellum Bowling Hall of Fame collection*

pinboy and flung behind a barbed-wire fence at an internment camp. When he was freed after World War II, Shimada was shunned by bowling clubs and leagues because he was Asian. Japanese American bowling leagues formed and featured Fuzzy as their champion bowler.

While both the NNBA and the Japanese American leagues expanded after the war, many bristled at being considered half-citizens and half-bowlers. Protesters hit the streets in 1948 and waved placards that declared, "Let's Celebrate Lincoln's Birthday the American Way. Let All Americans Bowl." Taking a cue from punning bowling cartoons, some banners demanded, "A 'strike' at democracy = something we can't 'spare.' " Some protesters

played on these minorities' valiant service during the war: "Chinese, Filipinos, Negroes, Hawaiians, Japanese. We had them 'strike' against the Nazis. Why not 'chalk up a strike' against discrimination. Let all Americans bowl!"

With a concerted protest from both the International Ladies' Garment Union and the United Autoworkers, who threatened not to support ABC's leagues, the ABC caved to pressure and outlawed discrimination from its tournaments.

Now that all races were welcome at the lanes, mainstream bowling magazines ran features on these newcomers, but not always with the most delicate language. *The Woman Bowler* of April 1963 wrote about Betty Jo Faust, who bowled 300, but used the questionable description

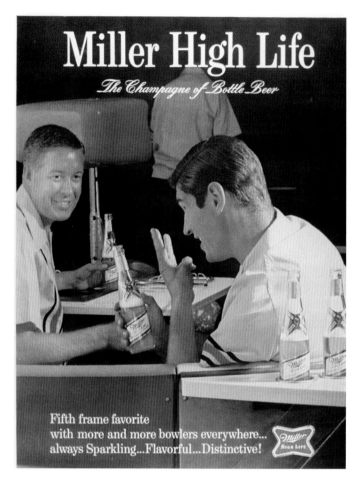

BEER FRAME Whoever has the lowest score by the fifth frame has to pony up and buy beer for the rest of the team. In this 1967 ad, one bowler teases a teammate about how many drinks he has to buy. *Shellum Bowling Hall of Fame collection*

BOOZE AND BOWLING While a couple of beers can loosen up the bowlers, just imagine what a bottle of whiskey can do. Better keep the kids at home. *Shellum Bowling Hall of Fame collection*

"Full-Blooded Indian" in the title. Even so, bowlers now all had equal rights and minority bowlers proved their worth, such as today's Paeng Nepomuceno from the Philippines who has won four World Cup Tournaments.

Bowl for Health!

During the 1880s and 1890s, bowling was heralded as the cure-all for the oversized waistline. Matchbooks blared "Bowl for Health" for men and "For Your Figure's Sake!" for women. Postcards portrayed rotund men shaped like their balls stepping to the foul line to lose a few pounds.

Bowling was the new health craze. Even *The Journal of the American Medical Association* reported, "Physicians recommend bowling, for it exercises unused muscles of the body and can be played year-round."

Around this time, *The New York Sun* featured an article on the bowl-for-health fever that was sweeping the country. "Some men who care nothing for the fine points of the game but want to get up perspiration to take off superfluous weight hire an alley by the hour and roll balls as fast as they can without having the pins set up."

There's this about Coke...

Drink Coca-Cola
REG. U.S. PAT. OFF.

See EDDIE FISHER on "Coke Time" NBC Television twice each week.

It brings you back refreshed

Take those busy, active days at work or play. It's surprising what Coke will do. How completely it refreshes, how quick to lift sagging spirits, how sure to please the most exacting taste.

Yes, you'll find Coke the *perfect* refreshment... any time.

BOWLING FOR COKE
After Prohibition, soda pop producers struggled to hold on to their newfound bowling market. In this 1957 ad, pro bowler Eddie Fisher shows off his form and pushes his "Coke Time" bowling spot on NBC. *Shellum Bowling Hall of Fame collection*

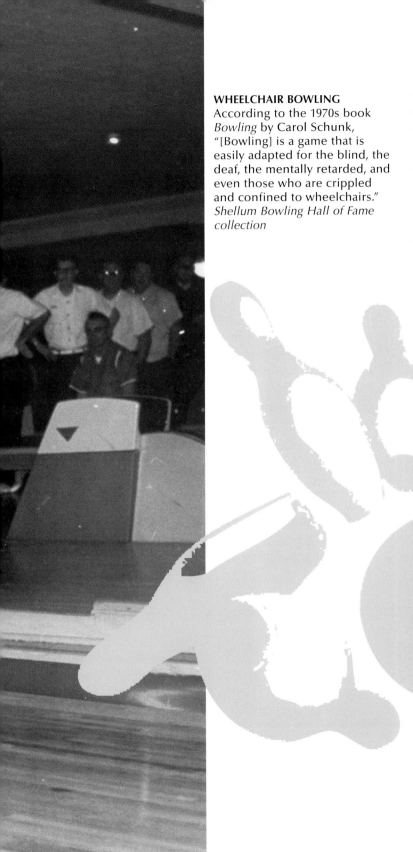

WHEELCHAIR BOWLING
According to the 1970s book *Bowling* by Carol Schunk, "[Bowling] is a game that is easily adapted for the blind, the deaf, the mentally retarded, and even those who are crippled and confined to wheelchairs." *Shellum Bowling Hall of Fame collection*

To encourage better health in 1910, "The YMCA provided health lectures and recreational programs which included bowling and baseball right inside factories," according to *City Games*. Enlightened corporations recognized that healthy employees are happy employees—especially if they can bowl.

Anyone could learn to bowl and one needn't already be fit. Not just brawny carpenters and burly factory workers, but "Thousands of workers in sedentary occupations find in bowling the means to get their much-needed exercise," according to Donald Casady in *Bowling* from 1962.

"Not for nothing has bowling become the greatest American indoor sport. It has a definite value as body exercise. There isn't a muscle, including those in your brain, that doesn't get a workout, and it has a decided value as a relaxer and a morale booster," wrote Joe Falcaro in his 1966 book *Bowling for All*.

Women were encouraged to join bowling's health revolution. The book *Better Bowling* from 1953 advocated bowling as the perfect exercise for the idle rich or the bored housewife. "[Bowling] was a wonderful thing for the women, too. Those who had been sitting at bridge tables day after day suddenly discovered that they could get a fine type of exercise which would allow them to keep their trim figures without effort."

As shown in *Bowling for All*, women bowlers were mostly respected for keeping thin, not their scores: "The story of Mrs. Flora D. McCutcheon, a Pueblo, Colo., matron who bowled for the express purpose of 'reducing a little' can best illustrate the rise of women in bowling."

Grandmother and champion bowler Marion Ladewig toured the country to promote her booklet "Bowl to Stay Slim" for women. Even so, most of the advocates for women to stay slender and sexy were men. Ned Hall pushed women to the bowling alleys in his 1948 book *How to Bowl*: "There is no question but that bowling is a great game for girls and women, as it promotes good posture, helps to keep figures trim, and being a group activity, develops and expands personality."

FEMININE BOWLING

In *The Woman's Bowling Guide* from 1959, Sylvia Wene includes an entire chapter on feminine hygiene and bowling. "A woman is known by the aura of femininity that surrounds her. Her perfume, feminine daintiness, and make-up help to make her even more lovely," she writes. Here are some of the highlights of keeping fresh while rolling a line:

• **Deodorants:** "Nothing spoils the illusion of feminine daintiness and, in a sport such as bowling, makes you feel more conspicuous than unsightly perspiration stains. Therefore a good antiperspirant and deodorant should be used. And not only under the arms, but this same antiperspirant should be placed at the bend of the knee and the crook of the arm."

• **Fragrance:** "A dusting of bath powder, followed by a very light misting of cologne over hair and body would not be overdoing it."

• **Hands and Nails:** "A sturdy manicure consists of a base coat, two coats of enamel, and a top coat....This builds up a shining protective coat of armor....To insure your hands against roughness, when you return from bowling be sure to apply a generous amount of hand lotion."

• **Make-up:** "Over the moisture foundation you may prefer a liquid foundation....This type doesn't streak or change color on the skin and is easy to use for touch-ups after you have finished bowling."

Suffragettes Strike

Despite being second-class citizens at the bowling alley and called "bowlerettes" by male bowlers, women persevered on the lanes. "When bowling with men, especially if you are a beginner, don't let their laughter bother you," advised *Bowling for All*. To avoid being distracted by unwanted attention and leering needlers, Spiezio made bowling blinders for women to keep their eye on the pins.

Women have been bowling since at least the mid-1800s, but were never welcome at the ABC. Not to be discouraged by this men-only league, women held their first national women's tournament in Milwaukee in 1905. Birdie "Kern" Humphreys of St. Louis, Missouri, won, ensuring herself a spot in the future women's hall of fame.

Seeing an opportunity to increase the number of bowlers on his lanes, alley owner Dennis Sweeney helped organize women's leagues and tournaments in 1907. Finally in 1916, the WIBC was born in St. Louis. Even though the women's suffrage movement wouldn't give them the right to vote until 1920, for now they could at least bowl on their own terms.

Women knocked down the pins with a vengeance, and in 1930 the first "sanctioned" 300 game by a woman was rolled. Many wives soon had a higher average than their husbands, and in 1966 Joe Falcaro wrote in *Bowling for All* that, "The ladies, moreover, take a much more enthusiastic attitude toward improving their scores than do the men."

"The thrill of competition was furnished to many of them for the first time in their lives," wrote Joe Wilman in *Better Bowling* from 1953. "The ladies are coming up fast in the bowling game now, and why shouldn't they? When you analyze it, the sport is a natural one for them, for it puts a premium on smoothness, gracefulness and rhythm, with which the average woman is born."

Male bowling journalists generally judged a woman's beauty along with her bowling technique, such as a lusty March 1965 article in *The Bowlers Journal* that Chuck Pezzano wrote about Jean Karamanos:

WHENEVER THIRST GETS IN THE GAME, HAVE THE

real thirst-quencher!

Nothing does it like Seven-Up

Thirst should be against the rules. And with 7-Up—it is! A bottle of sparkling 7-Up gets rid of thirst like nothing else can. Quickly—so thirst won't interfere with your fun. Completely—so that when you finish the bottle, your throat feels cool, your mouth feels fresh. You're ready to roll!

"FRESH UP" WITH SEVEN-UP

DATE NIGHT Soft drink 7-Up upped the ante against Coke by adding a young woman to its bowling ads. According to this 1958 image, bowling has become a wholesome activity for teenaged couples—a far cry from earlier in the century when most people thought of alleys as smoke-filled dens of sin. *Shellum Bowling Hall of Fame collection*

"Jean is a pretty miss, and had she strolled the area when Washington was there, he undoubtedly would have turned his head for a second look. In fact, she's a living, luscious answer to the critics who place women bowlers one notch above female shot putters when it comes to femininity. Oh yes, once you get past that pretty face, you find she can bowl—real well."

Be really refreshed! Bowl with Coke! Only Coca-Cola gives you the cheerful lift that's bright and lively... the cold crisp taste that deeply satisfies! No wonder Coke refreshes you best!

Tune in "The Adventures of Ozzie and Harriet" each week on your local ABC-TV station.

for THE PAUSE THAT REFRESHES

FAMILY AFFAIR After 7-Up included young women in its bowling ads, Coke brought in the whole family in this ad from 1960. The bowling alley was now deemed a safe haven for all ages—as long as bowlers drank Coke, not beer or 7-Up. *Shellum Bowling Hall of Fame collection*

Perhaps growing tired of being judged first on their figure and not their form, a magazine called *The Woman Bowler* debuted in 1936. An April 1963 issue reported that a survey from the WIBC found, " 'Mrs. Typical Bowler' is married to a league bowler and they have at least two children who are, or soon will be, in AJBC

[American Junior Bowling Congress] competition. She owns her own ball, bag, and shoes and purchases a new bowling blouse nearly every season."

Bowling alleys recognized women as a lucrative market. Female bowling teams garnered sponsors from jewelers, florists, and other women-focused businesses. While the traditional *Bowlers Journal* remarked in March 1965 that, "It isn't easy to draw a woman, even a woman bowler, from home and hearth," bowling centers had already created nurseries to watch over baby bowlers while the mothers had some fun. "Free coffee, free childcare, free bowling lessons," was the mantra of alleys looking to lure in some daytime customers. In the 1950s, the 19th Ave. Bowl in San Mateo, California, provided daycare for 75 to 100 babies per day. The Suburban Lanes in Buffalo, New York, had "wall cribs" that folded out to hold a newborn while rolling a strike. The All-Star Bowl in Skokie, Illinois, boasted "BABY-SITTING BY TV" with a television camera that pans through the nursery and feeds the image to closed-circuit monitors adjacent to the lanes. Women had successfully proved that they belonged in the bowling alley and proprietors would do almost anything to keep them there.

Today, the WIBC is the largest sports organization for women in the world. Along with the AJBC, bowling found a new audience and rapidly expanded. To honor the women who made bowling open to all (although the WIBC was white-only until 1950), a Women's International Bowling Hall of Fame was built as part of the bowling museum in St. Louis. A glass-enclosed display of a cobblestone from St. Louis marks the spot of the WIBC's founding, with this simple explanation for the brick, "It is significant because the WIBC started here in 1916." The museum features rows of oil paintings with portraits of women—mostly from the Midwest—who earned a coveted place in this hall of fame. In the background, a tape plays the sweet sounds of pins being knocked over amidst rumba lounge music.

JUNIOR BOWLING LEAGUES Poised to bowl strikes, these 10-year-olds met at the now-defunct Aqua Bowl where the family-friendly atmosphere resisted brewers' push to sell suds. *Hageman collection*

BOWLING DAY CARE This AMF promo photo shows how the most modern alleys offered nurseries to look after Junior while Mama bowled. Beware of any daycare that offers heavy wooden pins to toddlers as a toy!

LET'S GO BOWLING

Member BOWLING PROPRIETORS' ASSOCIATION OF AMERICA

CARSON CITY BOWL
FREE PARKING
NORTH CARSON ST,
GR. 2-9916
BRUNSWICK AUTOMATICS

CLOSE COVER BEFORE STRIKING MATCH

BOWLING'S FUN FOR EVERYONE

BRING THE WHOLE FAMILY!

BOWL WHERE YOU SEE THIS EMBLEM

BP AA

DIAMOND MATCH DIV. CHICAGO, ILLINOIS

OLYMPIC BOWLER At the 1936 Olympics in Berlin, Hank Marino showed the world what a graceful game bowling could be—and he cleaned house with all of his competitors. Despite Marino's efforts, bowling still isn't officially sanctioned by the Olympic Committee. Marino cashed in on beer endorsements, as in this 1949 ad, but his fame couldn't keep the bowling hall of fame in his hometown of Milwaukee.

"MAGIC TRIANGLE" This AMF ad pushed complete "AMF bowling accessories" that included clothes, bags, balls, and, most important, the air-conditioned lanes where the whole family could gather to cool off. *Shellum Bowling Hall of Fame collection*

BOWLING POP From Strike Soda to Bud pins, soda pop makers went to war with brewers to attract bowlers to drink their product during the fifth frame. *Shellum Bowling Hall of Fame collection*

REGULAR BOWLER With the "bowl for health" craze well underway, Saraka laxative hopped on the bandwagon because "sitting isn't exercise." What better way to slim down than laxatives, and "[t]here's no purging action, or violent irritation to whip intestinal muscles into shape."

WELL-ENDOWED BOWLERS As the butt of numerous bowling postcards and matchbook covers, hefty keglers took the "bowl for health" mantra to heart. These matchbooks ran sandpaper over the oversized derrieres of the drawings to strike the match. *Shellum Bowling Hall of Fame collection*

Exercise helps keep her **Regular...**

WHAT ABOUT YOU?

Does your daily work rob you of time for healthful exercise? If so, perhaps you need Saraka, to help you keep regular.

You know how it is . . . tied down all day to household chores . . . or sitting at an office desk. Then in the evening you sit some more . . . in the movies, at bridge, or just reading. And sitting isn't exercise.

This lack of healthful exercise can often leave you with a sluggish system. And when intestinal muscles get out of the habit of properly doing their normal work, they may become lazy.

Saraka can relieve your sluggishness the modern scientific way, with its *happy combination* of two pure vegetable ingredients. They work smoothly together to help you

SARAKA
REG. U. S. PAT. OFF.

FOR CONSTIPATION

SARAKA CONTAINS
TWO PURE VEGETABLE
INGREDIENTS:
BASSORIN AND FRANGULA

NET CONTENTS: 10 OUNCES

MADE IN U.S.A.

Distributor *Union Pharmaceutical Co.* Incorporated
BLOOMFIELD · NEW JERSEY

Ask Your Doctor

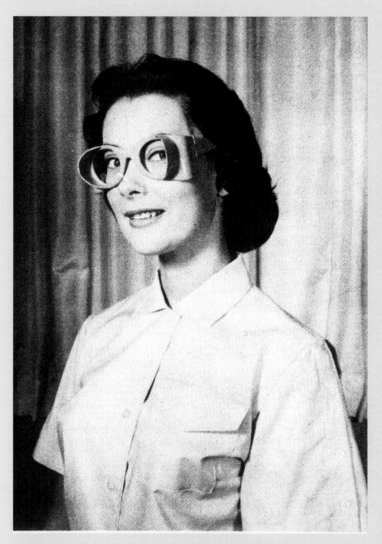

POWDER PUFF

Singles

BOWLING BLINDERS When leering men and nosy needlers attempted to spoil a woman's game, she could simply pop on a pair of these slick Spiezio bowling blinders from the late 1950s.

BOWL FOR HEALTH! After World War II, there were more desk jobs than ever and workers worried that their paunch would expand with their wallet. Alleys encouraged bowling as a way to shed those pounds. After the game, why not have some home-cooked burgers and a beer to wash it all down? *Shellum Bowling Hall of Fame collection*

BOWLING COWGIRLS When the Women's International Bowling Congress (WIBC) met in the Southwest, this dynamic duo knew they were in the Wild West and dressed the part.

65

CHEESECAKE MATCHBOOK COVERS
In the early days of bowling alleys, women were considered a sight diversion, particularly when pictured on matchbook covers in clothes that are falling off. Little by little, they were welcomed without catcalls when they bowled in leagues. *Shellum Bowling Hall of Fame collection*

WELCOME WOMEN
After years of cheesy soft-porn matchbooks, some alleys finally printed matchbooks that would appeal to women. Jumping on the bowl-for-health bandwagon, women were encouraged to shed the pounds while knocking down pins. *Shellum Bowling Hall of Fame collection*

PROPER BOWLING ETIQUETTE

Pamphlets, books, and brochures spelled out how to be an upstanding bowler by remembering your manners and obeying the polite protocol of the lanes. Culled from the pages of bowling literature of how courtesy is contagious, here are rules to bowl by:

- Never two-ball a pinboy. Don't fire another ball down the lane before the first one has been returned to you. You might injure the pinboy, and you are sure to make yourself mighty unpopular with those around you, even if you don't hurt him. Remember, if the pinboy should be injured, you might find yourself liable for damages.

- Never needle an opponent.

- Never say an opponent's shot was "luck."

- Do eliminate dilly-dallying between shots such as annoying and time-wasting motions as scraping of the feet, endless drying of the hands, and interminable posing when getting ready to make your shot.

- Do restrain your "bench jockeying" when your opponent is preparing to shoot.

- Be neither a moaner nor a braggart for neither attribute will win you any bowling friends.

- Mind your bowling manners. Fouling frequently brings on loud and unpleasant grumbling, in itself a breach of etiquette.

- Don't knock down the building with blazing speed, just knock down the pins.

- If you are a spectator, do not heckle the players, and if you are a player, do not lose your temper and use abusive language when you miss a shot or wind up with a pesky split...the pins can't hear you.

- When your average starts slumping, don't panic, don't get discouraged, don't throw your ball in the nearest river.

Chapter Four

"MAKE THAT SPARE!"

As the most popular participant sport in the country, bowling was a natural for the small screen. Cultural critic Marshall McLuhan wrote in *Understanding Media*, "Television demands participation and involvement in depth of the whole being. It will not work as a background. It engages you.... TV is, above all, an extension of the sense of touch, which involves maximal interplay of all the senses." How could bowlers not be engaged when nearly every one of them aspired to be a bowling star and they'd see ordinary people win fabulous prizes live on television? By watching bowling shows, any casual bowler could imagine the weight of the ball, feel the air blowing over the bowlers' hands to evaporate the sweat, slide subconsciously to the foul line, and share in the triumph of a strike. Bowlers watching bowling is a sensual experience because they know how it feels.

Early television needed sports programming. Filming football and baseball was too difficult for stationary cameras and too dull to watch for the audience. In 1947, the first bowling tournament was broadcast in New York from the Capital Health Center. The game was only shown locally, but the repercussions rippled across the country.

The contained indoor sport fit easily into the camera lens and foul weather couldn't postpone a tournament. The cameraman panned across the audience, closed in on the perspiration dribbling down the bowler's forehead, and zoomed to the end of the alley to witness the crashing pins. Television and bowling were a match.

NBC's Championship Bowling, hosted by Chris Schenkel from Chicago, was the first nationally broadcast show beginning in the 1950s and ran steadily for 15 years. *Make That Spare* and *Bowling For Dollars* soon followed. In 1961, ABC broadcast the PBA's tournament for the first time. *The Professional Bowlers Tour* became the second-longest-running sports

LAVERNE AND SHIRLEY By day the duo worked in a brewery; by night they met on the lanes. *Laverne and Shirley*, a spin-off of *Happy Days*, was based in Milwaukee—the land of beer and bowling.

series on television and soon merged with the *Ladies Pro Bowlers Tour*. Bowling stars, such as Dick Weber, Don "St. Louis Shuffler" Carter, Hank "Bowler of the Half-Century" Marino, and LaVerne "the Blonde Bombshell" Haverly, were made overnight.

With all the attention given to bowling VIPs, movie stars were jealous. To remedy the envy, hometown mixed with Hollywood to form *Celebrity Bowling* featuring such superstars as Ernie Borgnine, Bobby Darin, and Cesar Romero. On September 19, 1960, NBC followed with *Jackpot Bowling,* hosted by Mr. Television himself, Milton Berle.

Bowling's television popularity spawned spin-offs. WKRC in Cincinnati has the dubious distinction of being the first radio station to transmit bowling over the airwaves. From Betty Boop to Fred "Twinkletoes" Flintstone, cartoons used bowling for hijinks because the heavy balls easily replaced falling anvils and everyone knew the rules. "Virtually every cartoon has used a bowling theme," according to bowling expert Doug Shellum. Inspired by the lascivious antics of LaVerne Haverly, who paraded her sexuality on the lanes, the sitcom *Laverne and Shirley* featured two single women who spent a lot of time at Pizza Bowl, the bowling alley that Laverne's father owned. This theme would be revived 25 years later on the television show *Ed,* which featured a lawyer who owned an alley.

By the 1980s, television bowling began a steady decline from its zenith as the most-watched sport in America in the 1950s and 1960s. Cable television has since revived this made-for-media spectator sport that fits so well on the little screen. Bowling on television still inspires viewers to dream of being participants in the tournament as they can feel what the telecast bowler is

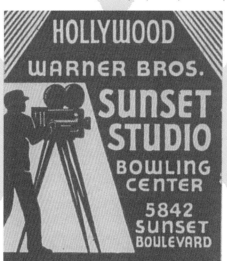

LIGHTS, CAMERA, BOWLING! Riding on the coattails of Tinseltown, the Sunset Studio Bowling Center hoped to attract movie stars to its lanes—or at least spread rumors that they might visit. *Shellum Bowling Hall of Fame collection*

experiencing, or as Marshall McLuhan pointed out, "The effect of TV [is] the most recent and spectacular electric extension of our central nervous system."

Knocking Pins on the Silver Screen

"You can apply everything that I've taught you about bowling to your daily life. And if you do that, you're gonna be decent. You're gonna be moral. You're gonna be a good man," says a father to his son in *Kingpin*. The child, Roy Munson (played by Woody Harrelson), disobeys his father by trying to hustle a priest and loses his bowling hand in the ball return. When you turn on bowling, you may never recover.

Bowling is its own reward in movies. While knocking over pins, everyone is happy in Hollywood. Heaven must have millions of lanes. One of the earliest lighthearted bowling shorts, *Strikes and Spares,* features trick bowling with a gaggle of buxom Bette Davis clones and a black-faced pinboy. Other early films starred Pete Smith in MGM's *Bowling Tricks* and Al Schacht (the clown prince of baseball) in *Bowling Alley Muscle Men.*

The first Tinseltown bowling celebrity was Andy Varipapa, whose trick bowling was legendary and required no film deception. Born in Italy, Varipapa boarded a ship for Brooklyn where he landed a job making door hinges. A movie mogul had Varipapa sign on the dotted line after he witnessed Varipapa's famous "boomerang ball" that skidded down the lane like a normal ball but stopped halfway and rolled back to him. Another trick involved rolling two balls simultaneously, one in each hand, that would make an "X" halfway down the alley and convert a 7-10 split. For a follow-up, Varipapa could cause his ball to hop the median between lanes and smash the pins for a strike next door.

In Dick Van Dyke's 1967 *Divorce American Style,* bowling provides the metaphor for the battle of the sexes. The lovelorn star chats with a bowling ball and introduces it to a pin as he tries to understand why women and men bowl each other over.

In Michael Moore's 2002 movie about gun control, *Bowling for Columbine,* he discovers that the two teenaged assassins delayed their shooting spree until after their favorite morning class: bowling. The killers had hoped to hijack planes in Denver afterward and crash them into New York. Perhaps more bowling classes could keep the youth of America—and the world—happy.

The best expression of bowling Americana in recent memory is the Coen brothers' 1998 *The Big Lebowski.* Walter, John Goodman's character, dumps out a Folger's coffee can to scatter the ashes of his friend Danny, but the remains blow all over his bowling partner, the Dude. Walter summed up what is important in life when he eulogized their dead friend, "Danny was a good bowler and a good man. He was one of us. He was a man who loved the outdoors. And bowling. Danny loved bowling."

Bowling, the Great Leveler

Just as bowling helped win World War II, it became an ad hoc symbol and rallying point during the Cold War. To prove that he was one of the people—and profess his love for the sport—President Harry Truman installed a bowling alley in the basement of the White House in 1947. Truman privately loathed the stuffy White House and called it a "glamorous prison," "the taxpayers' house," and "the great white sepulcher of ambitions." By adding an alley, Truman brought this sacred symbol of our government down to earth, and the mostly candid shots of the president bowling surely helped his re-election in 1948.

Also in 1947, the same year the Truman Doctrine was set in motion to contain communism, President Truman posed for the cover of the June edition of the bowling magazine *The National Kegler.* Immediately after World War II, politics pushed bowling into the

THE BIG LEBOWSKI

Marshall McLuhan wrote, "The movie is not only a supreme expression of mechanism, but paradoxically it offers as product the most magical of consumer commodities, namely dreams." In this European advertising poster, we see how the ultimate dream is that of bowling—when on a date with Wagner's Brünnhilde.

front lines of the Cold War with stakes that were nothing short of global annihilation.

The opposing media of the two countries—and the governments of the United States and Union of Soviet Socialist Republic—began the battle to portray their own people as the fittest, strongest, and most athletic. With rigid state control and perhaps some numerical adjustment, Soviet propaganda won the first battle and declared that more of their comrades played sports. In the 1963 book *Soviet Sport,* a quick recalculation by U.S. statisticians invigorated with the zeal of McCarthyism found, "In fact, more Americans engage in sports than Russians. We have over 20 million bowlers...." Suddenly, bowling's star rose as it gained status as a bona fide sport, on par with more physically challenging sports such as hockey, soccer, and track and field.

STRIKES AND SPARES With the booming popularity of bowling, MGM filmed this short in 1934 with 10 beautiful women and a black-face pinboy.

While the Russians used Marxist theory to indoctrinate the proletariat, Americans used the bowling ball to rally the masses. Italian communist Antonio Gramsci underestimated the working class by writing from prison, "The proletariat is less complicated than might appear." Nikita Khrushchev banged his shoe on the podium of the United Nations and declared, "We will bury you!" Khrushchev later explained that he meant the workers will rise and bury the capitalists.

Assuming that the American masses would rise up against the bourgeois, Marxist theorists ignored the power of bowling to break down class barriers—at least in the minds of bowlers. *The Literary Digest* wrote, "For unlike nearly every other sport, bowling tolerates no hypocritical distinction between professionals and amateurs." Bowling is the great leveler.

The 1966 book *Bowling for All* took the idea a step further. "[Bowling] is a means of relaxing everybody, professional men and women, and ordinary clerks, as well as a fine competitive sport that keeps the body and mind trim." The communist ploy of organizing American workers to revolt was foiled as the ultimate pastime kept their minds on the pins. Bosses bowled with their employees—a cynic would say to keep on eye on them—and, for a brief time, the most esteemed person was the one with the highest bowling average, not the biggest paycheck.

Bowlers had no need for Khrushchev's bricks and barricades when they had their balls and pins. Who wouldn't prefer drinking beer and hanging out with friends to staging a coup d'état? Or as punk band The Replacements would later sing, "The rich are getting richer, the poor are getting drunk."

In his book *Bowling,* Lou Bellisimo shares this punk cynicism. "...[M]any workers gain little or no satisfaction from their job. Since they spend about 40 hours a week on the job, anything that might make those hours more satisfying or meaningful might be worthwhile. Bowling is ideal as an employee sport."

During the Cold War, new immigrants flooded into the United States in search of the "melting pot." They imagined that they'd be cleansed of ethnic barriers and realize the American Dream with a bit of elbow grease. This promise of a better life could take generations, but luckily immigrants had the lanes to keep them happy. Approximately one-third of alleys during the Cold War were owned by foreign-born citizens, according to *City Games.* As citizens of the world gathered together to roll a few lines, bowling became the embodiment of the American melting pot.

Rather than tightening their collective belts to aspire to a Soviet state, most of these new American workers wanted a piece of the pie. While Cadillacs and Corvettes were pipe dreams, a shiny new bowling ball, hand-stitched bowling shirt, two-tone shoes, and a Naugahyde bag were within their economic reach. *Life* magazine reported in 1947 that the 18,500,000 people who bowled in the United States spent $200 million annually on bowling-related items. Capitalism and consumerism may have won over some of the workers, but the pie-in-the-sky pipe dreams often remained unattainable. Regardless, the accessibility of bowling to everyone knocked down barriers in this New World, at least in the alley. As part of bowling's marketing campaign, bowling shill Joe Falcaro declared in his 1966 book *Bowling for All,* "Bowling is the most democratic sport in the world because everybody plays it on an equal footing, and because of its wide range, it is open to everybody. The cry of 'Set 'Em Up,' has definitely become America's family battle cry."

BOWLING BOTH-HANDED
MGM tried again to tackle the subject of bowling by signing up Pete Smith for a short with zany bowling hijinks.

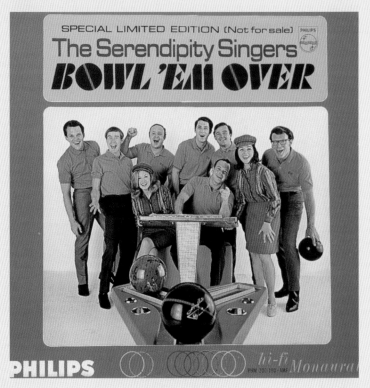

STEREO High Fidelity Album No. 6001

AMF PRESENTS

MUSIC FOR SWINGERS

Dedicated to the
millions of swingers
in the United States and
all over the world who
regularly enjoy the fun of bowling

Bowling brings out the SWINGER in you, too!

MUSIC TO BOWL BY Let's Go Bowling is a modern ska band, but the musical name stems from the 1930s sheet music of the same name. Other contemporary bands such as J. Geils Band, Foo Fighters, and Camper Van Beethoven used bowling motifs to spur their bands to success. Earlier, Don Carter gave his bowling advice on the patriotic-sounding disc *Spares and Strikes Forever*, the Serendipity Singers released their harmonic *Bowl 'Em Over*, and the pinsetting company AMF put out some swinging singles because "Bowling brings out the Swinger in you, too!"

BOWLING MAGAZINES While some sport magazines come and go, bowling remains a consistent seller—at least in the pro shops in bowling alleys. While esoteric compared to such giants as *Sports Illustrated*, the *Bowlers Journal* is the oldest sporting magazine in the United States, and possibly the world.

BOWLING IN MAINSTREAM MAGS Apart from numerous covers of the New Yorker, bowling was splashed across magazines covers, especially in the 1930s and 1940s. If women weren't bowling, at least they were beating men, as Irene is doing to Joe on the Saturday Evening Post cover. *Shellum Bowling Hall of Fame collection*

Volume 30, Number 13   Wednesday, November 24, 2004

METRO BOWLER "I started the Metro Bowler on a dare," recalls founder Pat Holseth. "A guy said a publication on bowling in this area couldn't work. I went to the University of Minnesota and got every book on journalism I could. I gave myself five weeks to turn a profit, and here we are 30 years later." Now the Metro Bowler is one of the five oldest bowling publications in the country. Pat's wife, Juette, took over as editor after one year and says, "We love the sport and we'll do anything we can to support the game."

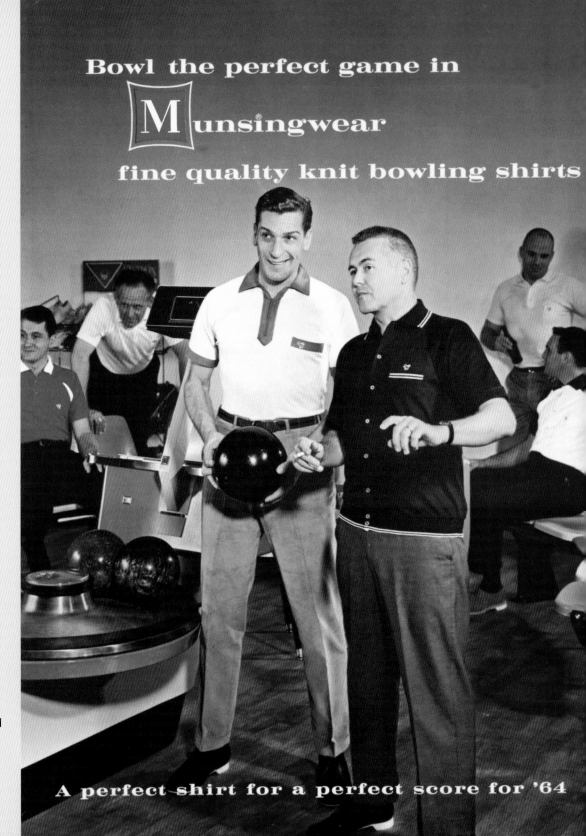

Bowl the perfect game in Munsingwear fine quality knit bowling shirts

A perfect shirt for a perfect score for '64

GOLLY, THINK I CAN CONVERT THAT SPLIT?
Having made a mint with the best itchless union suits in the nation, Munsingwear jumped on the bowling bandwagon with a line of his and hers outfits adorned with their trademark penguin. Here a pair of butch buddies share advice in their perfectly ironed shirts that have far too much cotton in the weave to get that clammy feel of a classic bowling shirt.

BOWLING STAMPS Across the world, knocking over pins has been honored by stamp societies dedicated to bowling philately. Even Cuba declares on its bowling stamp that "In socialist Cuba sport is practiced by the People." *Shellum Bowling Hall of Fame collection*

THE PRESIDENT BOWLER After dropping the bomb, Harry Truman installed a bowling alley in the basement of the White House in 1947 to unwind after a hard day of rebuilding Europe. Ever since Truman's terms, the White House bowling alley has represented the presidents' connection to the people.

SEE DICK BOWL To show his human side, Tricky Dick used to bowl in the White House basement. (No word yet on whether he taped his bowling banter with J. Edgar Hoover.) As a sort of presidential emissary for bowling, Nixon visited the world's oldest alley in Edinburgh, Scotland. Years later, George W. Bush bowled in the White House lanes but misjudged the approach and fell flat. In self-deprecating humor, Bush showed a slide of his Gerald Ford–like fall at a White House dinner when heavy-metal singer Ozzy Osbourne was visiting.

83

The 6th Annual

PUNK ROCK

Bowling Tournament

Feb 6-8, 2004
Castaways Bowling Center Las Vegas, Nv

FEATURING

Flogging Molly
Throw Rag

PUNK ROCK
KARAOKE

AT THE HOUSE OF BLUES

MANIC HISPANIC
in the cantina

LUCKY-13

In the Lounge

Harvey Sid fisher & Flock Of Goo Goo

PUNK ROCK BOWLING Every year in February, Las Vegas hosts the Punk Rock Bowling Tournament sponsored by BYO Records in Los Angeles. For three days, the famous Vegas Strip sees mohawks, piercings, tattoos, and sometimes impromptu amateur stripping contests along the lanes of Sin City. *Mark Stern collection*

REVOLUTIONARY ANARCHIST BOWLING LEAGUE Armed with bowling balls from thrift stores, the Revolutionary Anarchist Bowling League (RABL—pronounced " rabble") protested U.S. imperialism and chucked the balls through the window of a military recruiting station. What policemen would want to meet a group of anarchists rolling bowling balls down the street? This *RABL Rouser* newspaper was an early political 'zine to promote their politics.

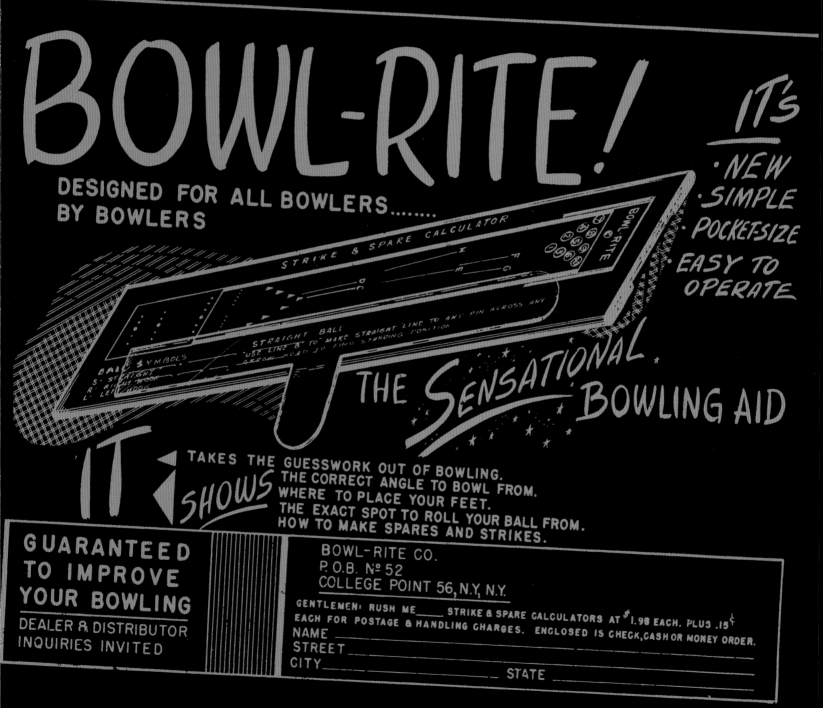

DEVIANT BOWLER As "an analysis of the human condition as seen through the eyes of a bowler," Julian Davis began his bowling 'zine called *Baby Split Bowling News*. Inspired by *Mad Magazine*, *Baby Split* had a new theme each issue with everything from a "Sci-Fi issue" with an alien space station diorama in the form of a bowling ball to a "New Age issue" with crystals to put in bowling ball finger holes for good luck. Davis began his love of the game when "Friends in punk rock bands stopped hanging out and got married, so we started going bowling and formed a club. We started going through the yellow pages and went to all the bowling alleys in alphabetical order." The high point of the 'zine was setting up a lane on a frozen Minnesota lake for "Ice Bowling." The fun stopped when the pinboy rolled back the ball and it kept rolling all the way across the lake. When the printing press stopped for *Baby Split* in 1995, Davis began work on two new 'zines: *Office Supply Junkie* and *Deviant Bowlers of America*.

When Tim Scott retired from *Mystery Science Theater 3000,* he had a vision that the people needed more bowling. Scott convinced Steve Sedahl, his coworker from the Cable Value Network, that Sedahl should host a comedy bowling show called *Let's Bowl.*

The color commentary was provided by Rich Kronfeld, previously known as Doctor Sphincter for his uptight anal-retentive personality. His new bowling nom de plume for *Let's Bowl* was going to be "Wally Bunghurt, but that didn't fly with Comedy Central, who changed his last name to Hotvedt," Sedahl says. Wally's bizarre and often dark commentary carried the show beyond mere slapstick. "Wally was obsessed with World War II and threw in all sorts of references to Blitzkrieg and specific warships when bowlers were knocking down pins," Sedahl says of his partner. "I would just say, 'OK ...That's great, Rich.' "

In keeping with the odd nature of the show, the two co-hosts took two of their biggest fans out for a night on the town for "Fan Appreciation Night." The camera focused on a shirtless Wally sticking out of the limo screaming in drunken revelry. The group goes back to Wally's girlfriend's house, but Wally and his girlfriend end up in an uncomfortable lovers' quarrel. The evening ends up at Wally's cousins' house listening to the police scanner for fun.

The actual bowling of *Let's Bowl* often resolved disputes between two parties who lacked the funds to go to court in a segment called "Grievance in the Gutter." Whoever won the game won the lawsuit. One case of marital strife involved a woman who didn't want any more kids and her husband who didn't want a vasectomy. When he lost the bowling game, a doctor's appointment was scheduled.

During *Let's Bowl,* special pins appear as the head pin for lucky contestants. If a strike is rolled in these tense situations, the bowler is awarded fabulous prizes such as the "Herring of the Month ...What's that? Hard of hearing? No, I'm hard for herring!"

More informative features included "Inside Bowling: How to Dispose of a Bowling Ball." Some of the questionable advice recommended throwing the ball into the woods, putting it in a newspaper machine, dropping it in a porta-potty, painting it like a soccer ball (but don't let dad accidentally kick it), throwing it in the lake (but don't be caught by the park ranger), or placing it on the exhaust stack of an outhouse (and backing away while it explodes).

Let's Bowl debuted in 1995 and ran until 2002. Comedy Central often airs reruns.

Chapter Five

BOWLING IN STYLE

Rolling Rocks

Rolling stones were the original bowling balls used in outside clay, wood, or grass lanes. Not only did they gather no moss, but they inspired an electric folk song by Robert Zimmerman, a band featuring a singer with oversized lips, and a well-known music magazine espousing a life of drugs, sex, and rock and roll.

The first bowler to move beyond rolling a rock and carve a ball out of wood is unknown. What has survived through bowling archives is the early wooden balls that are usually made of a very hard American tree called *lignum vitae*. The finger holes could be easily drilled into the wood, unlike the stone variation.

Clever bowlers carved extra holes in the balls and filled the holes with lead to give the ball a vicious hook. These balls were dubbed "dodo" balls by upright bowlers who saw no need to bamboozle other bowlers by debatable methods.

Another questionable trick by sly bowlers was to meld half of a 7-pound ball with half of a 9-pound ball. Western bowlers used these dodos in a match with eastern puritan bowlers. The UBC *Bowler's Journal* from New York called foul and nicknamed the bogus balls "bunco." Before the standard weight of between 6 and 16 pounds was established, some bowling balls weighed up to 30 pounds. "Especially Chicagoans" were blamed for using 22-pound balls to bend tournament rules in their favor.

In 1905, the first rubber ball was introduced. The "Evertrue" reduced noise in the alley and wear on the wooden lanes. Brunswick leaked that the Evertrue was made of a "mysterious rubber compound" called "mineralite," as though another chemical should be added to the periodic table of elements. Brunswick began mass-producing the Evertrue in 1914 and their fortune was soon made.

MERMAID S HOUSE BALLS The blinding neon paint, the multicolored tile, and the garish back-lit Plexiglas steps make the perfect combination for "cosmic bowling" at the Mermaid Bowling Center in Mounds View, Minnesota.

General Motors' concept of planned obsolescence didn't apply to bowling balls. The damn balls were so hard that they wouldn't wear out for years. Obsolescence of function was deemed almost impossible, so ball makers had to concentrate on obsolescence of desirability and made other colors and designs. While "house balls" were generally basic black, new mineralite balls came in multi-colored kaleidoscopic swirls.

When bowling became a popular sport among women and children, bowling ball manufacturers responded with the lighter "Lady Brunswick" and the "Junior Mineralite" series. Colors such as "Lollipop," "Grape," and "Blueberry" tempted the youth market, while women went for the "Lady Grabber" in psychedelic pink and turquoise swirls. Ads recommended that consumers eventually move up to a heavier ball, and support their favorite bowling ball company.

Bowling books, such as Ned Hall's 1948 *How to Bowl* advised, "You should, if you are rather plump or short, have your own bowling ball as soon as possible, as you will probably need a very narrow span with finger-holes of good proportions." Fitting the ball perfectly to your hand was deemed essential to improving your game.

BOWL YOUR OWN BALL! When the International Bowling Association met in Minneapolis in 1933, the back cover of the schedule booklet pushed its members to avoid the house balls with this early Brunswick ad. *Shellum Bowling Hall of Fame collection*

Although bowling balls were thought to be indestructible, the rubber and plastic balls absorbed oil from the lanes and the bowlers' hands. The ball's tacky surface would become covered with dirt and dust. A thin resin coat was applied to the next generation, and polyester or urethane sometimes offered a better covering to grip the wooden lanes for a wild hook ball. Microscopic shards of glass or ceramic were sometimes thrown in the mix to cover professionals' balls for the highest possibility of hitting the pocket.

Brunswick and other makers experimented with the balls' covered core for maximum punch against the pins. A barium center was the heaviest, but a ceramic core didn't absorb the shock as much and could transfer the hit to knock down even more pins.

Modern ball technology has lit up the lanes. Neon "day-glo" balls gleam electric during black-light cosmic bowling. Clear resin can turn a bowling ball into a time capsule to store anything from a skull to a hand grenade to Bill Murray's red rose in *Kingpin*. Today's bowling ball as an eyeball or the yin-and-yang symbol bears little resemblance to the medieval stones rolled in the town square.

Skirts, Shirts, Bags, and Shoes

"Show your good taste! Choose a color-coordinated Brunswick ball, bag, and shoe ensemble," advised Brunswick ads. Expanding on their line of balls, bowling companies offered a wide array of bags to match any outfit or mood. Bags came in "GTO Black" with racing stripes for the muscle-car speedsters; "Torino Chianti" for the Italophiles who don't know that Chianti is not from Turin; "Banner, red-white-blue" for the flag-waving patriots; and "avocado" to match 1950s kitchens.

BRUNSWICK S BEAUTIES A smattering of the color schemes in the 1960s shows that psychedelia stretched beyond Woodstock and into the local lanes.

Lolli-pop, Blueberry
$29.95

Lady Grabber
$29.95

Starfire II
$24.95

Crown Jewel, Blue
$23.95

Dropping a ball on the way to the alley, especially in a hilly area, could lead to damaging results; therefore, ball carriers were essential for bowlers who didn't use the house balls. The earliest ball bags were little wooden crates with leather handles sticking out of the top. When the heaviest 30-pound balls were outlawed, leather bags became de rigueur for the chic set in the 1920s. Cheaper vinyl, leatherette, or canvas were deemed strong enough for the bowling bag heyday of the 1950s and 1960s.

The next item to fulfill the wardrobe of any self-respecting bowler is the shoes. For the perfect gliding form, chalk was rubbed on the bottom of bowling shoes. Much to the chagrin of alley owners, nails protruding from the leather soles left gouges in the approach. To preserve the slick wooden slats, alleys began renting house shoes as part of the payment of bowling a line.

By the 1920s, the rubber sole was introduced to stop the sliding bowler from crossing the foul line. For right-handers, the left shoe slid while the right shoe with the rubber sole stopped the slide.

Bright two-tone shoes replaced high-topped leather boots with thin soles and a dozen eyelets. The new multi-colored suede or leather shoes matched the bag and the ball. Perhaps as an attempt to expand the new shoe market, women bowlers were warned in the 1966 book *Bowling for All,* "Do not attempt to bowl wearing high heels or crepe-soled shoes." Special fashions for women were marketed, such as bowling socks with a "nylonized" heel and toe to prevent wear and a "puff cuff" bobby sock that rolled neatly over the ankle.

In the late 1990s, fashion houses in Milan co-opted the 1960s bowling vogue by remaking bags and shoes and

LONG LIVE THE DODO! Around the turn of the nineteenth century, bowling enthusiasts started using the name of the bizarre Dodo bird—extinct since the late 1600s—to mean a strangely weighted ball that would do vicious hooks and curves. Many bowlers used Dodos for trick bowling; a wobbly ball could perform marvelous maneuvers down the lane. In this 1940s ad, Brunswick claimed the name Dodo for its new machine to make the old Dodo extinct.

who says the DODO is extinct?

You bowl a better game because of it!

This Brunswick craftsman intends to weigh each portion of a Mineralite bowling ball—top, bottom, and sides! Neat trick? Yes, but he'll do it with a Dodo, the curious yet precise scientific instrument shown here.

Small matter that this Mineralite has been tested for balance many times before. It must be checked again upon the Dodo so that it will always roll as you direct it. This is Brunswick craftsmanship . . . A proud, never-satisfied craftsmanship. One that has made the Mineralite America's favorite Bowling Ball.

● Order to your measure at all leading bowling establishments, credit jewelers, sporting goods stores, department stores, Brunswick Salesrooms. Your choice of 4 colors in regulation A.B.C. weights.

"Healthy" balls have a sound all their own. Here, Brunswick craftsmen bounce each ball, listen for the sound variations that tell of any hidden defect.

Copr. 1940 by The Brunswick-Balke-Collender Co.

Brunswick
CUSTOM-FIT
MINERALITE BOWLING BALL

slapping on their designer labels for their leggy models to wear on the catwalk. This resurgence in bowling style caused a rash of used bowling shoes thefts. Juette Holseth, owner of the West Side Lanes in St. Paul, Minnesota, said in 2005, "Nowadays all the kids want the bowling shoes, so we make them leave their ID or something valuable. We used to just take their street shoes, but sometimes they'd leave us their ratty old shoes that they didn't want anymore."

The other much-sought-after items are classic bowling shirts. The earliest bowling garb was sleek silk shirts or thick turtleneck sweaters because the lanes often lacked heat. "The Cleveland armory, where the 1904 ABC was held in the dead of winter, was so badly heated and the roof was so leaky that ice formed on the lanes from melting snow, and the shivering competitors had to bowl in heavy winter gear," according to *The Big Book of Bowling*.

Audiences at early tournaments were almost entirely men in formal three-piece suits. Competitors were allowed to remove their jackets and hats when knocking down pins.

After World War II, the ideal bowling shirt was designed with extra pleats under the arm for more freedom and better form. Brand names such as Hilton, Nadine, Crown Prince, King Louie, Weber, and Hale-Niu specialized in bowling shirts with a loose collar that rarely buttoned up. The stitched logos that adorned the back of the shirts from the 1950s and 1960s were often sponsored and inevitably funny. Bowlers' creativity shined when given free reign to design an outrageous team emblem.

Tailors sewed the early shirts out of cotton, rayon, gabardine, challis, linen, or satin. By the 1970s, the chemical generation made their colorful shirts out of clammy polyester, sheeting, poplin, and staticky polyester blends.

Women's fashion took advantage of these new manmade materials, but bowling style went high class. "Here's high fashion in bowling in the form of a coral wool jersey dress. The skirt unbuttons to reveal matching pants," according to one bowling ad from the 1960s. A groovier advertisement recommended, "These hip-rider pants, matched with a peppermint-striped cotton 'grand daddy' shirt and sleeveless zip jacket, is a bowling fashion as chic as any you will find."

Comfort on the lanes was paramount for women as ads warned, "Be certain the bowling clothes you select offer lots of freedom of movement. Skirts should have extra pleats." In fact, the special " 'Slaxskirt' was a short slack and skirt all in one" and was designed exclusively for bowling women. *The Woman's Bowling Guide* warned women not to wear suggestively skimpy outfits and replicate the embarrassing cheesecake paintings of beautiful women falling on the lanes. This 1959 guide for women recommended, "Women's skirts had extra pleats," and one said, "Too many women attempt to bowl in tight, binding skirts which prevent them from striding properly."

Some women may have followed these fashion tips, but at the 1964 WIBC in Minneapolis, few followed this "sensible" advice. *The Woman Bowler* from April 1963 reported, "the Western Amusement team of Missoula will wear Indian uniforms. The Liberty Majors team will also dress in Western attire.... Leather skirts, vests and headbands will be the special feature of the Lakeroad 'Rawhides' team of Neenah, Wisconsin...the Artistic Beauty Salon team of Brainerd, Minnesota, will wear pastel-colored hair." Bowling style showed that truly anything goes in the alley.

Long Live Bowling!

After dips during the Depression and World War II, bowling's popularity peaked in the 1950s and 1960s. According to *Bowling Alone*, "At the peak in the mid-1960s, 8 percent of all American men and nearly 5 percent of all American women were members of bowling teams."

By the end of the 1960s, bowling's popularity slowly seemed to unravel. "Practically all the major pro teams disbanded, and the sport's two biggest competitive events were halted: the World Invitational in 1965 and the BPAA All-Star in 1970," according to *The Big Book of Bowling*.

Cougar
$12.95

Mojave
$11.95

Rogue, Black-White
$9.95

Lolli-bag, Blueberry
$9.95

Desert
$7.95

Newport
$7.95

Colony-Red
$5.95

Colony-Black
$5.95

Tournament
19.95

Executive
14.95

Caravelle, red, also in
avocado and black **13.95**

Mustang blue,
also in black **9.95**

Silhouette raspberry
7.95

Silhouette tapestry
7.95

GTO butterscotch
Also in white, red or blue

GTO black

Prophets predicted that the bowling apocalypse was nigh. In fact, the opposite was true. More people were packing the lanes than at any other time in history— only not in leagues. According to *Bowling Alone*, "...more Americans are bowling than ever before, but league bowling has plummeted in the last 10 to 15 years. Between 1980 and 1993 the total number of bowlers in America increased by 10 percent, while league bowling decreased by more than 40 percent."

The cultural studies book *Bowling Alone* theorizes that America has fallen from being a society focused on participation to one of the individual. The catchy title, *Bowling Alone*, is deceptive, however, because although people may not bowl so much in leagues, they rarely bowl alone.

This premise is confirmed by Pat and Juette Holseth, the owners of West Side Lanes, "Declining number of lines bowled can partially be blamed on cable TV and kids' outside activities. Bad news is league numbers are down. Good news is open bowling is up."

Open (or casual) bowling has kept the lanes in business, but owners are often nervous because leagues used to guarantee a full alley every day. When enthusiasts lacked the commitment to a league, bowling buddies dubbed them "habitual bowlers," with the underlying message that they can't quite break the habit.

Alley owners have searched to expand their market to all ages. "Date Night" bowling caters to love-struck couples too shy to cozy up except when teaching each other proper bowling techniques. Black lights, glow-in-the-dark balls, and Day-Glo planetary landscapes on the walls lure in teenage bowlers for "cosmic bowling." Raucous rock bands set up on the side of the lanes to serenade disgruntled youth during "Rock-n-Bowl." Baby bowlers have bumper bowling so pesky gutterballs won't cause tantrums.

BOWLING BAGS The ball matches the bag that matches the uniform. Any self-respecting bowler has his or her own ball, and the bag shouts the fashion statement. From GTO racing bags to carpet bags, Brunswick offered styles for executives to housewives.

With this new renaissance, "Bowling is the most popular competitive sport in America. Bowlers outnumber joggers, golfers, or softball players more than two to one, soccer players (including kids) by more than three to one, and tennis players or skiers by four to one," according to *Bowling Alone*.

Bowling shills at the ABC estimated that 91 million Americans bowled in 1998, compared to a paltry 73 million who voted that year. The message is more Americans bowl than participate in the electoral process. Impartial statisticians approximate the number of bowlers much lower, at around 54 million. With bowling's popularity sweeping through Latin America, Canada, and Asia (especially Japan), more than 100 million people bowl each year. Across six continents and in more than 90 countries, bowling has earned the crown of the most popular participatory sport in the world.

BOWLING HATBOX Not only were bowling ball bags de rigueur, but WIBC hall-of-famer Sylvia Wene brought her bowling hatbox to the lanes.

READY TO ROLL After World War II, bowling uniforms resembled off-duty soldiers more than the polyester beauties of the 1960s and 1970s. *Shellum Bowling Hall of Fame collection*

LEISURE SUIT LEAGUE While bowlers may not have worn their matching leisure suits on the lanes, they wore the best threads of the 1960s and 1970s for their photo shoots. *Shellum Bowling Hall of Fame*

TIE ONE ON Bowling ties let keglers show their passion for their favorite pastime even at formal affairs. *Shellum Bowling Hall of Fame collection*

SHOES TO BOOT Early bowling boots were often basic black and laced up the ankle to avoid any unexpected twists on the rough lanes. By the 1950s, two-tone shoes matched the brightly colored shirts and the high-finned Chevys in the parking lot. *Shellum Bowling Hall of Fame collection*

Every man needs GABANARO...

the sports shirt with perfect fit--now "Sanforset" for permanent fit, longer wear.

IF YOU had to pick *just one* sports shirt— it would have to be Arrow *Gabanaro!*

For one thing, it's the sports shirt that can be worn with *any* sports outfit. *This alone* wins it thousands of new friends every week.

Made of a rich, durable rayon gabardine, *Gabanaro* is WASHABLE, available in a wide range of popular colors, features the new ARAFOLD collar that looks great ... *feels* great ... open or closed, with or without a tie! $6.50.

EXACT COLLAR SIZES!

EXACT SLEEVE LENGTHS!

another smartly styled

ARROW

TRADE ® MARK

SPORTS SHIRT

Cluett, Peabody & Co., Inc.

NO WRINKLES EVER! The miracle material of rayon gabardine made even the roughest game of bowling seem like a formal affair. Bowling shirt manufacturers took the advice to heart and used the synthetic fibers to make wrinkle-free shirts and never mind if the bowler stays clammy underneath the shirt. *Shellum Bowling Hall of Fame collection*

KING LOUIE As one of the many bowling-shirt brands, King Louie offered the coveted bowler stitched into the collar. Other styling cues included bowling pin buttons that never worked quite as well as they looked. *Shellum Bowling Hall of Fame collection*

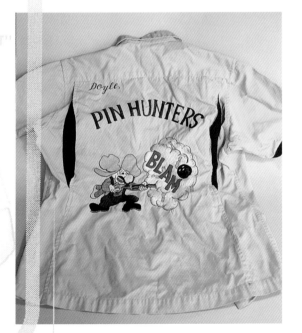

BLAST THOSE PINS! Clever and colorful embroidered backs of bowling shirts were the envy of fellow bowlers on the lanes. Scores may determine winners, but whoever has the best shirt wins. *Julian Davis collection*

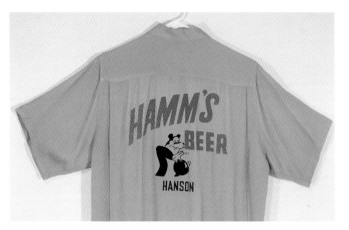

BEER TEAM SHIRTS Breweries were eager to sponsor bowling teams as long as their logo could be emblazoned across the back. *Shellum Bowling Hall of Fame collection*

ALL-STAR TEAM Local pros had slick stitched logos embroidered across the back of their shirts. Now these uniforms are coveted by collectors. *Shellum Bowling Hall of Fame collection*

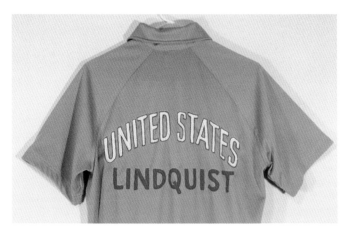

TEAM USA While it is still not officially recognized as an Olympic sport, bowling does have its International Bowling Federation, or Federation Internationale des Quilleurs (FIQ), to give the sport legitimacy the world over. *Shellum Bowling Hall of Fame collection*

Time out for Pepsi—
the *Light* refreshment

If you're interested in averages—observe the looks of the average modern woman. She's trimmer, she's slimmer, because she prefers lighter, less-filling food and drink.

Pepsi-Cola—the modern, light refreshment—fits right in with her sensible diet. Today's Pepsi, reduced in calories, is never heavy, never too sweet. Wherever you play, say "Pepsi, please," and refresh without filling.

Pepsi-Cola refreshes without filling

BOWLING SKIRT
Pepsi showed how women could keep trim and fashionable with an outfit to make any date ogle with awe. The moral of the ad? Bowl for health and drink Pepsi for the "sensible diet" for the "average modern woman" who is "trimmer [and] slimmer." *Shellum Bowling Hall of Fame collection*

I dreamed I bowled them over in my *maidenform bra*

SWEET MUSIC*...dreamy new Maidenform bra...spoke-stitched cups for gently rounded curves—newest you-est way to look. Laminated undercups for never-let-you-down uplift! 2.50. Also Sweet Music Full Length. From 3.95.

BOWLING BALL COIFFURE BY LAURENCE OF ULTIMA   *REG. U. S. PAT. OFF. ©1961 BY MAIDENFORM, INC.—MAKERS OF BRAS, GIRDLES AND SWIMSUITS

1961 BOWLING WONDER BRA Years before sport bras allowed women to comfortably participate in athletics, Maidenform pushed its brassieres to female bowlers in order to comfortably roll some rocks.

GUSSIED UP IN GUSSETS

Taking advantage of the bowling craze sweeping the country, Susquehanna pushed its "Ship 'n' Shore" outfit for the female bowler in this 1948 ad in *Life*. Within just a few years, bowling magazines had full spreads of the latest style on the lanes. An August 1961 article in *Popular Bowling* proclaimed, "Light and bright are the fashion shades this season. The 'fruit' shades are especially prominent not only in the latest fashions from Paris, Rome, and New York, but also in the beautiful new styles for bowling."

SHIP 'N SHORE

'Bowling is its forte, but it's tops for every sport! Sanforized broadcloth ... action-back gussets ... long long tails ... $3.

SUSQUEHANNA
1350 Broadway, New York 18

FLASHY FLORALS Just as men had their leisure suits for team photos, women bowlers had their matching dresses made out of slick wrinkle-free fabric.

AHOY! Bowling magazines, which were usually written by men, advised women on slim and sexy styles that brought out curvaceous lines thanks to short skirts and tight blouses. Fiddlesticks! Women wore outrageous outfits thanks to this newfound freedom given to them by bowling. If men could have glitzy bowling shirts, why couldn't women?

BOWLING MOBILES The Bowling Pin Car was built in 1949 around a 1936 Studebaker Coupe frame by Mike Skrovan. Today, the mobile pin rests in the basement of the International Bowling Museum in St. Louis. The House of Balls art car was created by sculptor Allen Christian as his daily driver.

97 - Early Bird - 98
"Pinata"
Fran Sm...

LEAGUE CHAMPS 68-69

TROPHIES GALORE Marble, brass, and varnished wood made up the fancy awards for bowlers, but the bigger the size the bigger the victory. Now that forgotten bowling trophies can be snatched up at the local Salvation Army, classic car enthusiasts pop one on the hood for the best ornament in town. *Shellum Bowling Hall of Fame collection*

Champion Hamm's Beer Team -- Hamm's Beer Bowling team of the Minneapolis Traveling League has tied the second highest American Bowling Congress Regular Division score in history to win the ABC National Team Championship. Holding their championship trophy are (left to right): Bill Baden, Gordy Dahl, Bob Hanson, Glen Olson, and LeRoy Bryant.

BOWLING MEDALS From tie clips to key chains and earrings to brooches, bowling medallions usually consisted of mini molded balls and pins to show the wearer's love of the sport. Each ABC tournament has a new medal that eager bowlers buy up as a memento and instant collectors' item. *Shellum Bowling Hall of Fame collection*

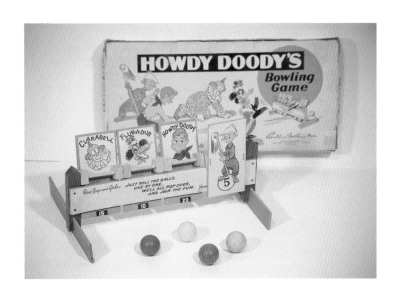

CHILDREN S GAMES A millennia before Christ, the Egyptians developed a child's bowling game. Today, toddlers and teens alike are enchanted by miniature bowling toys. *Shellum Bowling Hall of Fame collection*

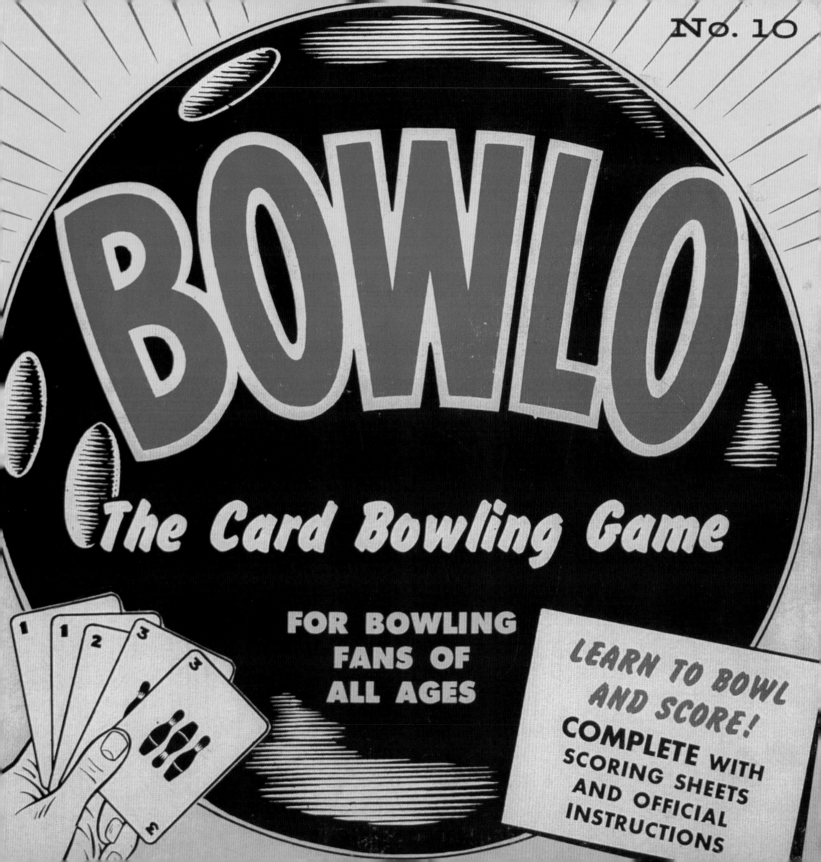

114

HOUSE OF BALLS

Eerie music seeps out of the doors of a sculptors' gallery in the warehouse district of Minneapolis. Red-and-white pins dangle precariously from the ceiling as though they are ready to bop visitors on the head. Dim lights focus on strained faces carved into the flesh of abandoned bowling balls. This is Allen Christian's House of Balls, named for his penchant for grinding bowling balls into fabulous busts of tormented or placid people.

"I just call up bowling alleys for balls and I leave with a truckful," Christian claims. "I've got bowlers that come to drop 'em off, but I can't even use them all."

Christian's brand of found object art has kept his sculpting going for 24 years and the House of Balls alive for 18 years. His balls have toured other states and 10 U.S. embassies in Africa for an art show about reusing and recycling materials.

Even Christian's pickup truck has been the victim of his bowling obsession. It is adorned with plastic red bowling pins and "House of Balls" written along the side in shoe soles. He's driven the bowling car across the country, but "only in Minneapolis have I been ticketed. Cops hate the red lights on it, as if only their cars can have red lights." The bowling car was the star at the annual Art Cars on Ice on frozen Lake Minnetonka in 2002.

Just as Michelangelo insisted on choosing his own marble at the Carrara quarries, Christian has his own predilection for bowling balls. "You know they have balls with gyroscopes inside of them. I prefer the old balls, though." The different colorful layers used to construct a bowling ball add to the expression on the faces of his sculptures, but Christian usually doesn't know what he'll find inside a ball until he carves it open.

The floor around a bowling sculpture work-in-progress in House of Balls is covered with powdery ball shavings. Christian worries about the effect of inhaling bowling ball dust over the years and shows me his new ventilation system for grinding. Still he worries about the delayed effects of being a bowling-ball sculptor and theorizes, "It's my own feeling that the balls are probably repositories for nuclear waste."

PINBOWL To increase profits and enhance entertainment, alleys soon added soda pop machines, video games, and pinball machines. After spending the evening bowling, what better way to unwind than play bowling pinball? *Shellum Bowling Hall of Fame collection*

BARROOM BOWLING When a tavern couldn't afford a true lane, a Majestic Bowler or other makeshift bowling game took its place. *Shellum Bowling Hall of Fame collection*

BOWLING FENCE Outside the famous Amana Colonies in Iowa stands an old farmstead in Marengo with bowling pins atop the fence posts all around the yard. Perhaps an escapee from the German utopian cooperatives discovered the beautiful experience that is bowling.

PAUL AND BOWLING BABE Where Paul Bunyan Land used to stand in Brainerd, Minnesota, is now the home of the Paul Bunyan Bowl. The mammoth lumberjack rolls only strikes with his over-sized ball and Babe the Blue Ox chomps any pins left standing.

BOWLING BRIC-A-BRAC Bowling knickknacks run the gamut from flowerpots to salt-and-pepper shakers. When bowling paraphernalia was at its height in the 1950s, bowling prophylactics named "Spares" hit the market for couples who can't wait. *Julian Davis, Shellum Bowling Hall of Fame collection*

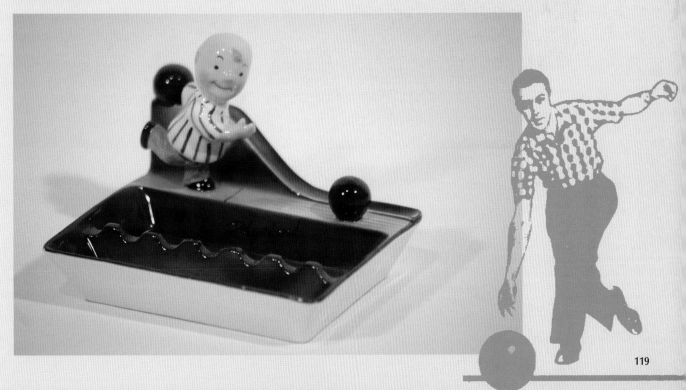

INTERNATIONAL BOWLING HALL OF FAME AND MUSEUM The International Bowling Museum originally opened in Greendale, Wisconsin, just outside of Milwaukee in 1973. "When St. Louis was awarded the Bowling Hall of Fame, many people thought that Milwaukee would never recover," according to native Milwaukeean Charlie Dee. The new state-of-the-art bowling museum in St. Louis that was built in 1984 has a winding display through the history of the sport with dioramas of Henry VIII and mannequin pinboys waiting to set up the fallen timber. At the top of the museum is the ABC Hall of Fame and the Women's International Bowling Hall of Fame. The men's side (pictured) has stately bronze plaques in muted light, while the women's has colorful oil paintings of the entrants under bright fluorescent lights. The final stop is the basement for free bowling (with admission) on renovated classic lanes that require pinboys and a couple of modern lanes.

anchor: the last bowler on a team to clean up.

apple: slang for a bowling ball.

baby split: a 2-7 or 3-10 split.

back-up: a right-curving ball (for a right-hander).

barmaid: a pin hidden behind another one that often isn't seen until the first one is knocked down; also called a "sleeper," a "double wood," a "tandem," or "one in the dark."

bedposts: a 7-10 split; also called "fence posts."

belly the ball: increasing your hook.

benchwork: distracting an opponent with conversation from the bench.

big ears: a 4-6-7-10 split.

blow: not making a spare.

board: the wooden planks of the lane.

body English: a bowler's form and praying after the ball has been released to wish the ball into the pocket.

bridge: the distance between the bowling ball's holes; also called the "span."

Brooklyn: when the ball sneaks over to the left side of the pins; also called a "crossover" or "Jersey."

cheesecakes: hot lanes that are easy to strike; also called a "soft alley" or "pie alley."

cherry: knocking down the front pins in hopes of a spare with the second ball; also called a "chop."

Christmas tree: splits that have the shape of a pine tree, usually a 2-7-10 or 3-7-10; also called "faith, hope, and charity."

Cincinnati: an 8-10 or 7-9 split.

creeper: a ball thrown so slowly that it barely strikes the pins.

crossovers: when a ball hits the pocket between the first two pins of the opposite side, e.g., a right-hander hitting the 1-2 pocket or a left-hander hitting the 1-3 pocket.

crow hopper: a slack hold on the ball.

curtain: the end of the game when the anchor (last bowler) doesn't make a spare in the tenth frame; also called "lights out."

curve: a ball that begins turning to the left (for a right-hander) the moment it hits the lane, as opposed to a hook that curves closer to the pins.

dead apple: when a ball strikes the pins but has no power to knock over many of them; also called a "flat apple," "water ball," or a "squash," and the opposite of a "honey."

dodo: a ball that is heavily weighted on one side to give a phenomenal, if illegal, curve.

double pinochle: a 4-6-7-10 split.

double pinochle with the ace of spades: a 4-6-7-10 split with the 9 pin as well.

drink frame: the fifth frame in which the bowler with the lowest score must buy beer for the team.

drive: the alley or lane.

Dutchman: scoring 200 by alternating spares and strikes in each frame; also called a "Dutch 200," a "sandwich game," or "the hard way."

flat alley: a lane that neither lets a ball hook nor stay straight (hold).

floater: a ball with no curve.

forestry: slang for bowling because a bowler knocks down wooden pins. (Your occupation? "I'm in forestry.")

foundation: scoring a strike in the ninth frame.

frame: each box on a score sheet amounting to one-tenth of the game.

goalposts: a 7-10 split.

golden gate: a split looking like the bridge, usually a 4-6-7-10 split.

Grandma's teeth: a split that looks like nothing except for a few old chompers.

grasshopper: a dynamite ball that makes the pins hop.

graveyard: an alley where scoring is difficult.

groove: a supposed dip in the alley boards that brings the ball into the pocket.

gutterball: when a ball rolls off the lane into the side gutter, amounting to a zero in the frame.

head pin: the number 1 pin; sometimes mistakenly called the king pin, which was an oversized pin in skittles.

honey: a great ball.

hook: a ball that curves at the last minute.

hook alley: a lane that carries the ball to the left (for a right-hander).

kegler: a bowler; from the archaic German word for bowling. (Early Germanic men supposedly carried a "kegel" or pin with them for protection.)

kindling wood: pins that fall over with ease.

king pin: the 5 pin in ten-pin bowling; originally, the tallest pin stuck in the middle in the Dutch game of skittles.

knocking the wood: hitting a lot of pins.

leave: the leftover pins after the first roll.

lily: a 5-7-10 split that is very difficult to clear.

lofting: holding on to the ball too long so it lands with a bang partway down the lane.

maples: another name for bowling pins because they're often made of maple wood.

mark: making a strike or spare.

mother-in-law: the hidden 7 pin in the corner; from the older pin game of "kankakee" or "five-back," where no score was given if the 7 pin wasn't toppled.

mule ears: a 7-10 split

Murphy: an easy split, or baby split, usually of the two pins almost in front of each other, e.g., the 1-6 or 2-7 pins.

nose hit: striking the 1 pin straight on.

open frame: no strike or spare in the frame.

part of the building: when the 7 or 10 pin is left standing after a good hit of the other pins.

picket fence: when a whole line of pins are left, e.g., the 1-3-6-10 or 1-2-4-7 pins; also called a "clothesline."

pocket: the area between the 1 and 3 pins for a right-hander and 1 and 2 pins for a lefty.

poison ivy: a 3-6-10 split.

poodle: another word for a gutterball.

powder puff: a ball thrown softly or an older term for the women's league; also called a "puff ball."

powerhouse: a strike that takes all the pins into the back pit.

pumpkin: a ball without much power or action.

railroad: another word for split; also called simply "rail."

sandbagging: bowlers keeping their league scores down to increase their handicap in tournaments, which can keep them banned for life from bowling.

schleifer: a strike when the pins fall slowly; from the German verb to *slice.*

slot lane: an alley with easy strikes.

snake eyes: a 7-10 split.

snow plow: a hook that sweeps the pins down; also called a "sweeper" or a "broom ball."

sour apple: when a ball strikes the pins but has no power to knock over many pins.

spare: knocking down all pins with two balls.

spiller: a strike in which the pins fall slowly; also called a "sweeper."

splash: a strike that sends the pins flying.

strike: knocking down all pins with one ball.

striking out: a good move, unlike baseball, in which the bowler finishes the game with all strikes.

tap: throwing a ball that seems like a perfect strike but leaves a pin standing.

telephone poles: a 7-10 split; it can also mean pins that won't fall.

throw rocks: make strikes.

turkey: three consecutive strikes.

umbrella: scoring a strike from hitting the 1 pin straight on.

woodcutter: a ball that breaks sharply and chops down the pins.

wooden bottles: slang for pins.

woodpile: the pins; also called "lumber" and "timber."

Woolworth: a 5-10 split from the five-and-dime store nickname; also called a "dime store" or a "Kresge."

BiBLiOGRaPHy

Baudrillard, Jean. *The System of Objects*. London: Verso, 1996

Barsanti, Rena A. *Bowling*. Boston: Allyn & Bacon, Inc., 1974.

Bellisimo, Lou, and Larry Neal. *Bowling*. Englewood Cliffs, New Jersey: Prentice-Hall Inc., 1971.

Burton, Nelson Jr. *Bowling*. New York: Atheneum, 1973.

Casady, Donald, and Marie Liba. *Beginning Bowling*. Belmont, California: Wadsworth Publishing Company, 1962.

Cruchon, Steve, Chuck Pezzano, and Bruce Pluckhahn. *Pins and Needlers*. South Brunswick, New Jersey: A.S. Barnes & Co., 1967.

Decker, Wolfgang. *Sports and Games of Ancient Egypt*. New Haven, Connecticut: Yale University Press, 1987.

Dulles, Foster Rhea. *America Learns to Play*. New York: D. Appleton-Century Co., 1940.

Falcaro, Joe, and Murray Goodman. *Bowling for All*. New York: Ronald Press Co., 1966

Hall, Ned. *How to Bowl*. Boston: Halcyon House, 1948.

Martin, Joan L. *Bowling*. Dubuque, Iowa: Wm. C. Brown Co. Publishers, 1966.

"Gutter Mouth: Pete Weber wants to make bowling the new wrestling." Ben McGrath. *New Yorker*, Sept. 23, 2002.

McLuhan, Marshall. *Understanding Media: The Extensions of Man*. New York: Signet, 1964.

Morton, Henry W. *Soviet Sport: Mirror of Soviet Society*. New York: Collier-Macmillan Ltd., 1963.

Reiss, Steven A. *City Games: The Evolution of American Urban Society and the Rise of Sports*. Urbana, Illinois: University of Illinois Press, 1989.

Schunk, Carol. *Bowling*. Philadelphia: W. B. Saunders Co., 1970.

Showers, Norman E. *Bowling*. Pacific Palisades, California: Goodyear Publishing Company, 1969.

Stallings, Howard. *The Big Book of Bowling*. Salt Lake City, Utah: Gibbs-Smith Publisher, 1995.

Steele, H. Thomas. *Bowl-O-Rama: The Visual Arts of Bowling*. New York: Abbeville Press, 1986.

Wene, Sylvia. *The Woman's Bowling Guide*. New York: David McKay Co., 1959.

Wilman, Joe. *Better Bowling*. New York: Ronald Press Co., 1953.

ACKNOWLEDGMENTS

Thank you to Allen "House of Balls" Christian; Julian "Baby Split" Davis; Carlotta and Alessandro Dradi for corrections on the finer points of table *bocce;* Hans Eisenbeis and Ruthann Godollei for tips on local bowling sculptors; Eric Hageman and his dad for Aqua Bowl R.I.P; Pat and Juette Holseth at the Metro Bowler; Rich "Dr. Sphincter" Kronfeld; Mort Luby and his bowling art; Piccola Katy McCarthy for believing that bowling is truly our salvation; Dennis Pernu for this great idea; Mike Schmid from Minnehaha Lanes; Tim Scott for dreaming up *Let's Bowl;* Steve "Chopper" Sedahl; Doug Shellum with his hall of fame goldmine; and Charlie "Pinboy" Sugnet.